P1

MW01614492

"What we need now more than ever is calm, intelligent voices urging us to see the lies and emptiness behind the claims that abortion is a woman's right, her choice, and for her good. Stephanie Gray Connors is a uniquely wise and winsome voice, and her message is desperately needed. Give a copy of *My Body for You: A Pro-Life Message for a Post-Roe World* to every abortion supporter you know—or anyone who needs clarity and encouragement in their pro-life work."

Lila Rose
Founder and president of Live Action

"In a society bloated with 'fearmongering misinformation' about our bodies, Stephanie Gray Connors shines a light of gentle truth and transforming mercy. From personal experience, Stephanie knows how difficult pregnancy can be and yet how beautiful are the loving sacrifices of mothers and fathers. I strongly recommend this timely book."

Bishop Emeritus Thomas J. Olmsted
Diocese of Phoenix

"This book is amazing! It's beautiful. Stephanie Gray Connors has provided us with pro-life messaging that is outstanding and deeply needed in this post-Roe world."

Kristan Hawkins
President of Students for Life of America

"In the wake of the pivotal reversal of *Roe v. Wade*, renowned pro-life apologist Stephanie Gray Connors presents *My Body for You*—a masterful work that rises above the legal and political fray over abortion. This book isn't merely a call to action; it's a deep, heartfelt challenge. Through riveting stories and insights from her years on the front lines, Stephanie reshapes the abortion debate, urging readers to recognize our inherent design for communion and love. *My Body for You* reignites the readers' passion for protecting life and empowers them to courageously and convincingly share this message with our society. It's no longer enough to merely change laws—we must also transform hearts, minds, and lives. We need this book now more than ever!"

David Bereit
Founder of 40 Days for Life
and host of The David Bereit Show

"Stephanie Gray Connors has debated (and toppled) leading pro-choice professors and was invited to Google's headquarters where she delivered a viral talk on abortion. But she's more than a world-class advocate and debater. As a woman and mother, she exudes compassion, warmth, and sensitivity. In *My Body for You*, Stephanie brings these many gifts to bear on the fascinating juxtaposition between the Eucharist and abortion, the sacrament of the Church and the sacrament of secularism, the two dominant paradigms on offer today. Using not only logic but also personal stories and touching anecdotes, she reflects on the meaning of our body to show how its ultimate purpose is to be a gift, not a death chamber. Read this book to understand the abortion question from the heart of a mother."

Brandon Vogt
Founder of ClaritasU and author of How to Discuss Abortion with Pro-Choice Friends and Family

---

"For my money, Stephanie Gray Connors is the greatest pro-life apologist in the English language. *My Body for You: A Pro-Life Message for a Post-Roe World* is classic Connors—watertight logic, lucid and engaging prose, and a message imbued with love. Read this book! It has the power to change one's paradigm in arguing *for*—and living *out*—the pro-life message."

Fr. John Parks
Priest of the Diocese of Phoenix

MY BODY
FOR YOU

MY BODY
FOR YOU

A **PRO-LIFE** MESSAGE
FOR A **POST-ROE** WORLD

STEPHANIE GRAY CONNORS

EMMAUS
ROAD
PUBLISHING

Steubenville, Ohio
www.emmausroad.org

EMMAUS
ROAD

Emmaus Road Publishing
1468 Parkview Circle
Steubenville, Ohio 43952

Library of Congress Control Number: 2023950142
ISBNs: 978-1-64585-361-9 Paperback | 978-1-64585-362-6 Ebook

Layout and design by Allison Merrick.

To my children in heaven (LaeLae, Michael, Ollie, and Job) and my children on earth (Violet and "Gio")—in expanding my womb, you have expanded my heart.

I appeal to you therefore, brethren, by the mercies of God, to present your bodies as a living sacrifice, holy and acceptable to God, which is your spiritual worship. Do not be conformed to this world but be transformed by the renewal of your mind, that you may prove what is the will of God, what is good and acceptable and perfect. . . .

Let love be genuine; hate what is evil, hold fast to what is good; love one another with brotherly affection; outdo one another in showing honor. Never flag in zeal, be aglow with the Spirit, serve the Lord. Rejoice in your hope, be patient in tribulation, be constant in prayer. Contribute to the needs of the saints, practice hospitality.

Bless those who persecute you; bless and do not curse them. Rejoice with those who rejoice, weep with those who weep. Live in harmony with one another; do not be haughty, but associate with the lowly; never be conceited. Repay no one evil for evil, but take thought for what is noble in the sight of all. If possible, so far as it depends upon you, live peaceably with all.

ROMANS 12:1–2, 9–18

Contents

Introduction

Where were you when . . . ?

That is a question we ask each other on the anniversaries of significant moments. People readily recall where they were and what they were doing when they heard about JFK's assassination, the death of Princess Diana, or 9/11. Associating our personal life circumstances with something that is momentous, earth-shattering, and historic is an indicator of the imprint a particular event can leave.

Where were you when the Supreme Court of the United States (SCOTUS) overturned Roe v. Wade? On June 24, 2022, after almost fifty years of widespread access to abortion across America—and the destruction of more than sixty million pre-born lives—SCOTUS handed down the Dobbs decision declaring, "The constitution does not confer a right to abortion."[1]

With a draft decision being leaked in May of that year and the close of the SCOTUS season the following month, pro-lifers expected the decision and were keeping vigil in

---

[1] Dobbs v. Jackson Women's Health Organization, 597 U.S. (2022), https://www.supremecourt.gov/opinions/21pdf/19-1392_6j37.pdf.

1

Washington, DC. When June 24 arrived, many were there at the Capitol to celebrate the historic decision. As for me? Although I had spent the previous twenty years working full-time in the pro-life movement, when that momentous day arrived, I was a new mom to my ten-month-old, and I was "keeping house." More specifically, I was cleaning the bathrooms. And when my husband saw online that Roe had been overturned, he informed me of that glorious fact as I was literally scrubbing a toilet.

As I wrote later for *Catholic Answers*, "I joined him in watching the news of what truly is an amazing part of history, which we are privileged to live through. I felt strangely content delighting in the news while being 'hidden' at home—not on the front lines, but reaching down to pick up my ten-month-old daughter and breast-feed her as I took it all in. To be a mother at that very moment made it all the sweeter."[2]

Then I noticed a text from my friend and fellow pro-life apologist Trent Horn. He wrote, "I'm grateful I could stand alongside you, friend, to play a small part in today's victory with our work. I know babies can be a lot of work, but we still need your gifts for the long road ahead."

Trent is most certainly correct that there is a long road ahead. A battle may have been won, but a culture war is still raging—stronger now than ever. In the year since the Dobbs decision, flames have been stoked and fires

[2] Stephanie Gray Connors, "A New June: Less Pride, More Life," July 4, 2022, https://www.catholic.com/magazine/online-edition/a-new-june-less-pride-more-life.

are burning. On the one hand, the judgment was most certainly a victory for the pro-life movement, as it took away the sacred cow of the abortion rights movement.

The Supreme Court's declaration that there is no constitutional right to abortion, however, pushed the subject back to the states. That means that while some states, like Alabama, have implemented protections for the pre-born, other states, like California, have doubled down on their support for abortion. Heated debates fill the internet. Pro-life organizations, pregnancy centers, and churches have been targets of vandalism and violence.

The Family Research Council kept a running tally of attacks in the first year after the draft Dobbs decision was leaked in May 2022, identifying over one hundred attacks on churches, pregnancy centers, and other pro-life organizations.[3] These included the dumping of dead animals on the property of a pregnancy center in what appeared to be a type of satanic sacrifice,[4] and the throwing of Molotov cocktails at a pro-life office, igniting a small fire.[5] Abortion supporters protested outside the private family homes of Supreme Court justices Amy Coney

---

[3] "Attacks on Churches, Pro-Life Organizations, Property, and People Since the Dobbs Leak on May 2, 2022," Family Research Council, last updated on May 19, 2023, https://downloads.frc.org/EF/EF22F17.pdf.

[4] Houston Keene, "Florida Pro-Life Pregnancy Center Targeted with Decapitated Chicken, Mutilated Lamb in 'Ritualistic Attack,'" Fox News, May 12, 2023, https://www.foxnews.com/politics/florida-pro-life-pregnancy-center-targeted-with-decapitated-chicken-mutilated-lamb-ritualistic-attack.

[5] "Police Identify Suspect Vehicle in Oregon Right to Life Break-In," KGW8, last updated on May 12, 2022, https://www.kgw.com/article/news/crime/molotov-cocktails-oregon-right-to-life-keizer/283-84ffd04a-41ba-47fd-99d9-7af4a61ddfde.

Barrett and Brett Kavanaugh. A man was even arrested for an assassination attempt on Kavanaugh.[6] People who feel threatened by an advancing pro-life position are bringing their very personal and emotional stories to the public square in an effort to reverse the reversal of Roe.

In light of this, as Trent alluded to in his text to me, I had to ask myself what we all should ask ourselves going forward: *How will I be involved? What gifts will I offer?* I paused at his words. I recalled a phrase often quoted from a poem long forgotten: "The hand that rocks the cradle is the hand that rules the world."

Having a busy, two-decade long career and then becoming a mother at the age of forty, I had a strong sense I had entered a new and sacred season. While I was still doing some pro-life work, I realized that how I mother my daughter will influence not only her future, but it will also influence everyone she encounters. The time and attention I give my daughter will leave an indelible imprint on her that will affect her indelible imprints on others. My main focus is her proper formation and flourishing. In 1865, William Ross Wallace wrote as much when he penned, in part,

> Woman, how divine your mission
> Here upon our natal sod!
> Keep, oh, keep the young heart open

---

[6] Holmes Lybrand and Tierney Sneed, "FBI Says Man Accused of Attempting to Kill Brett Kavanaugh Said He Was 'Shooting for 3' Justices," CNN, July 27, 2022, https://www.cnn.com/2022/07/27/politics/kavanaugh-roske-arrest-warrant/index.html.

Always to the breath of God!
All true trophies of the ages
Are from mother-love impearled;
For the hand that rocks the cradle
Is the hand that rules the world.

Of my essential part in my daughter's thriving I was well aware. So, too, was I aware of another reality—that of the many hands capable of rocking a cradle but unwilling to do so. By that I mean the many who would receive new lives in their wombs but end them before they would hear sweet lullabies. These would not be lives never lived. These would be lives brutally cut short. And the abortion of the youngest of our kind, if left unchallenged, will not only destroy unrepeatable and irreplaceable individuals. It will also leave a devastating impact on women, men, and all of society. For as William Ross Wallace also wrote,

Infancy's the tender fountain,
Power may with beauty flow,
Mother's first to guide the streamlets,
From them souls unresting grow—
Grow on for the good or evil,
Sunshine streamed or evil hurled;
For the hand that rocks the cradle
Is the hand that rules the world.[7]

---

[7] You can read the poem, "The Hand That Rocks the Cradle," in its entirety here: https://allpoetry.com/The-Hand-that-rocks-the-Cradle-Is-The-Hand-That-Rules-The-World.

Good or evil. Sunshine streamed or evil hurled. These are the options put before our world today. As my one hand rocked the cradle to bring about good and to stream sunshine, could my other hand write an appeal to our world to do the same? Could I put words together to convince the culture that life in a womb is as valuable and worthy of our investment as life in a cradle? This book aims to do that, to be a timely resource for people of goodwill to use as a type of manual to help them in the intense dynamic of this post-Roe world.

State by state, there are new abortion laws and new legal challenges for the pro-life movement. In every community, there are personal stories going viral that are pulling on heartstrings and leading some to believe that abortion is the answer to difficult life circumstances.

As the battle intensifies, we need a coherent and compelling message. Whether we debate abortion in a courtroom, in a state legislature, on social media, outside an abortion clinic, or in conversations with family and friends, we need to be able to articulate the philosophy driving pro-life initiatives in a post-Roe, post-Dobbs world.

For many years, including when I lectured at Google headquarters, I presented the pro-life message by "speaking the language of my audience," meaning if it was a non-religious audience, I would use non-religious arguments. During that same time, I encountered some pro-life people who believed that we needed to share the Gospel to convert people to Christianity, and once that was accomplished, the public would become pro-life.

It is not either-or; it is both-and. There is a place for meeting people where they are, addressing a particular subject of interest at face value. Winning someone over on the dignity of pre-born children specifically can *then* lead such an individual to ask deeper questions about why humans are valuable in general, and subsequently lead them down a path of deep spiritual conversion. Alternatively, there are many who come to know Christ who *afterward* readily accept that the pre-born are worthy of protection because they accept that God said humans are "very good," that God considers humans so valuable that we are worth dying for, and because God made us in His image. People can come to truth from different paths.

This book is designed to connect those paths. While providing a robust argument from my many years of experience debating abortion, this book also speaks to the religious truth that will ultimately set our culture free. It connects the Gospel of Life to the Gospel itself.

In his 1868 novel, *The Idiot*, Fyodor Dostoevsky wrote, "Beauty will save the world." That is what the Gospel— which means "the good news"—did. The *Good News* is beautiful, for it is a story of challenging circumstances, stepping into the unknown, being aided and supported, carried and comforted, of being banished and reunited; it is a story of self-sacrifice and of the greatest love of all. When we present that story as the heart of the pro-life message—for it is—its beauty, its power, its magnetism, *that* will change the world.

The need to communicate what I consider to be a more *holistic* pro-life apologetic, as outlined in this book, comes in part from my own experience of motherhood—its triumphs and trials. In the year since Roe was overturned, I lost three more babies to miscarriage. The fragility of life, of pre-born life in particular, has become very real to me. The devastating impact of delivering three dead babies in less than twelve months has shattered my heart. The fact that we are pilgrims on a journey, and this earth is not our home, has become abundantly clear to me through the loss of my little ones who have found their heavenly resting place. Communicating to our broken culture a life-giving message that is grounded in an eternal perspective has become more urgent to me.

That pregnancy is hard I know well. I am pregnant again. I live with tipping scales of excitement at a new child and dreadful fear of another miscarriage. And I write this on a day when morning sickness has overwhelmed and depressed my spirits. I have felt the looming pressure of this book's deadline, but all I could do while my toddler napped (prime writing time) was let my weary body succumb to its own naptime as well.

But somehow, someway (the grace of God, really), I have also learned that it is possible to push through that which is hard. And isn't that life? It's messy and challenging but also so beautiful. So here I am, a few hours later, eking out an opportunity to write some more.

In the pages that follow, I aim to share my experiences and insights as a debater, and now a mother, to provide a robust defense of the pro-life message while exploring the topics of pregnancy and abortion. Part apologetics, part memoir, part sharing the Good News, the hope is that my words inspire readers to a deeper level of love. For within the story of the greatest love—which began as a pregnancy—within our own stories of embracing maternity and paternity (whether biological or spiritual), we can unlock the ethos to move us forward in this post-Roe world.

As my one hand rocks the cradle, I want to use the other to give you, dear reader, a message to change the world.

What Are Our Bodies For?

"I should have been a nun."

That was my statement to my husband when I was in the throes of labor. At nine centimeters dilated, I was experiencing searing physical pain that was unlike anything I had known before. It was agony. It felt like torture. And I wanted it to stop. My declaration of desiring an alternative vocation to our marriage was really just another way of saying I wanted the suffering to stop—and I knew being a nun was a path void of childbirth. My words were amusing because although I had spent a season discerning religious life, I had longed for marriage for many, many years. In fact, when people would suggest the convent to me, I would respond by expressing my deep desire for marriage.

When humans are in pain, we say all kinds of things. My agony-riddled declarations continued: "I want a C-section!" I cried out. Ironically, the whole reason I was experiencing such brutal pain was because I chose an epidural-free labor out of concern that taking an epidural could increase my risk for a C-section. As I learned, pain causes us to say the darndest things.

During my pregnancy, I had taken a class to prepare for birth and learned that when a woman gets to the point of thinking she cannot endure any longer, that's usually when the baby is born. C-section wasn't medically indicated, nor, at that stage, was an epidural feasible. So as I was nearing the end of my twenty-four-hour marathon, I made a third declaration to my husband: "I want to die!" I cried out.

One of my fears before childbirth was that I would die in labor. Granted, that was highly unlikely to happen in the developed world, yet for some reason—the way people fear spiders or public speaking—I feared death while giving birth. That my fear before labor would become my *desire* in labor makes me marvel at what happens when pain overtakes us. No, I shouldn't have been a nun. No, I did not want a C-section. And no, I did not wish to die. The words I had strung together were my feeble attempt at communicating my actual wish: for the agonizing pain to cease.

In the weeks following, when I relayed this experience to a priest friend of mine, he responded by saying, "You did die. The old Stephanie is no more. Now that you are a mother, your whole life is transformed."

"Truly, truly, I say to you, unless a grain of wheat falls into the earth and dies, it remains alone; but if it dies, it bears much fruit" (John 12:24).

For the first two decades of my adult life, I traveled the world speaking and debating on the topic of abortion. My events were filled with controversy, and my job was never boring. I've stood before chanting mobs and required bodyguards. At some events, organizers arranged for armed police officers, and I was given security briefings and escape plans should my audience get out of control. At one venue, I even had to accept having an undercover police officer accompany me to the bathroom to ensure my safety.

Then there was the time during one of my debates on a college campus when an audience member released a stink bomb to try to get the room to clear so the debate wouldn't continue. Chanting and disruptive audience members were a regular occurrence and, on occasion, led to the suspension of my debates until order could be reestablished. I've been at events where abortion supporters physically assaulted my team members and property.

Although in my professional work of tackling the topic of abortion I have faced countless tests and trials, nothing could prepare me for the challenge of becoming a mother. Don't get me wrong—this admission of challenge should not be equated with regret. My life is the richest it has been since welcoming children into it, but in some ways, life has been the hardest since then too.

Over a period of twenty years, many abortion supporters asked if I had ever been pregnant. When my answer back then was no, it seemed to give them grounds to dismiss my views on abortion. It was as though they celebrated my lack of experience as a win for their position.

Logically, I knew I did not have to experience something in order to make an educated comment about it. I knew such a critique of me was a fallacy, an ad hominem attack—attacking who I was instead of what I argued. I knew that when abortion supporters did that, it showed weakness on their part, because instead of having the strength of argument to prove my claims wrong, they ignored my evidence and reason entirely and chose the path of dismissing me as a person. I knew that experiencing pregnancy was not necessary for my position to be valid. And yet, as with any issue, now that I have become a biological mother, I see how experience can *enhance* one's position.

Have you ever been sick for some time only to wake up one day feeling entirely better? Isn't the contrast powerful? Doesn't health taste wonderfully sweet when preceded by illness? That comes to mind when I think of the contrast between the agony of labor and the ecstasy that comes immediately after a child is born. My husband tells me the pushing portion of my labor lasted one and a half hours. I need to rely on his recollection because that was a blur to me. It felt never-ending. I pushed with whatever strength I could muster after a day, and while every push technically brought my child closer to my arms, each push *felt* like failure when she did not come out.

But then the final push came. And there are no words to adequately capture the utter euphoria of the sudden ceasing of all prior pain. With what seemed like extraordinary abruptness, it was finished. After nine months of experiencing the youngest of our kind growing within my womb, after a week of being ill with COVID-19 culminating in twenty-four hours of labor, my sweet one was suddenly on my chest.

Unlike many, my husband and I chose to wait until birth to find out if we had a boy or a girl. I would have been happy with either, but the name Violet Grace had come so easily to us that when the midwife declared, "It's a girl!" my now-empty womb was replaced by an overflowing heart that utterly delighted in the little flower being placed on my chest. I had warned my husband that it was common for babies to come out looking ugly, but she was the prettiest baby I'd ever seen.

I've learned that life is a series of joys and sorrows, of consolations and desolations, of ease and challenge. The tender moments of skin-to-skin between my baby and me acting as a reprieve from the brutality of labor was followed by the next challenge—breastfeeding. Many references have been made to the fall of Adam and Eve leading to increased pain in childbirth, but what are the origins of breastfeeding being so overwhelmingly difficult? Nursing did not come easy to me, and I was to learn many women share this harrowing experience. *Why is something so natural, and so necessary for a child's survival, so difficult?* I wondered that and wailed it in prayer more than once.

Having your hungry newborn scream at your breast that she refuses to latch onto is distressing. Weeks later, when that latch finally comes but brings with it enormous pain that leads to your breasts bleeding, you experience a whole new agony. *Why does it hurt?* I also wondered and wailed this in prayer.

A dear friend who was a few months ahead of me in her own roller-coaster ride of breastfeeding gave me hope. She encouraged me to not give up (which I was on the cusp of). She assured me the pain would go away and that nursing could be a beautiful experience.

Fast forward a couple months and we were finally in a groove. No more pumping. No more nipple shield. No more supplementing with formula. No more bleeding. No more pain. Just sweet moments of tenderness as my little one fed at my breast. Desolation. Consolation. Challenge. Ease.

One Sunday, when Violet was six months old, she began to fuss in church. Knowing that nursing was calming to her and that she was probably hungry, I opened my arms and my husband passed her to me. I sat down and offered her my breast. As I gazed upon my daughter's sweet face happily receiving my milk, I listened as the sacred liturgy continued. At the very moment in which Violet began to feed, our priest picked up a piece of bread that, like me, was to be transformed. He then reverently recited from the Scriptures,

> Take this . . .
> And eat of it,
> For this
> is
> my
> body
> which will be given up
> *for* you.

What I heard before me was living upon me. Words spoken two thousand years ago were alive in a new way. My very body, not only before birth but now after, was being given up for my child. She was literally consuming me. My body was my offering to her. It was, and is, my gift for her.

After so many years of talking about abortion and wading through argument after argument, it occurred to me that the very heart of the pro-life message is captured in that moment and in those words.

Those who promote abortion chant its opposite: "My Body! My Choice!" they demand. Pro-lifers typically point out that when a woman is pregnant, there is a second body present. We respond that a pregnant woman's body no longer involves her body alone, so we need to consider the baby's right to his own body too. But I think there is a more fundamental message we need to communicate, and it's something for us to propose as a question: What are our bodies *for*? It is a question that comes to mind when I recall perhaps one of the most significant debates of my career.

In October 2020, I debated controversial and notorious Princeton philosophy professor Peter Singer through an online event sponsored by groups at Harvard University. Having spoken of Singer's worldview to my audiences for two decades, training them in its pitfalls, it was an incredible opportunity to finally engage the man himself and to do so in front of a listening audience.

During my opening remarks, I told the audience that for forty years I had been a mother-to-be. People often misunderstand what that label actually means. No, I said, I hadn't been in a state of perpetual pregnancy. Precisely because I had *never* been pregnant for the first four decades of my life meant I had never become a mother; hence, I was a "mother-to-be" (assuming biological motherhood lay in my future, that is).

Indeed, I pointed out that several weeks before the debate, my very essence had changed; I had been transformed from simply being female to taking on the identity of mother—I became pregnant for the first time. Singer responded positively when I incorporated my exciting news into my remarks: "I'm delighted to learn that you're pregnant," he said in front of those tuning in. "Congratulations. I wish you all the best with that pregnancy."

Women aren't congratulated for having eggs in their bodies, so his positive response to the news of my embryo seemed to be an acknowledgment that there is something different—and special—about pregnancy. Indeed, in presenting his position on abortion, he acknowledged that the pre-born child is a living member of the species Homo sapiens. But his point was that this isn't relevant. In his mind, what determines whether a being is protected—has a right to life—is related to whether that individual has feelings, wishes, and desires.

What gives an individual moral status, in his view, depends on "capacities, characteristics and qualities that beings have."[1] Is an entity capable of feeling something,

---

[1] Peter Singer and Stephanie Gray Connors, "Resolved: Abortion Is Immoral," First Annual Dr. Mildred Fay Jefferson Symposium, sponsored by Harvard

such as pain? Do they have self-awareness? Are they beginning to develop desires and hopes for the future? In Singer's world, embryos and fetuses don't have plans, and he acknowledges infants don't either, thereby admitting he does not think infants have full moral status.

Singer said he has defended the rights of parents who have a disabled infant to pursue active euthanasia of such a born child. It is "not until sometime after birth that human beings have the full right to life that you and I have,"[2] he said. After the debate, an audience member e-mailed me saying,

> I've been wrestling with the sentiments Peter shared around suffering and humans with compromised capacities. Some of what he said greatly troubled me. What occurred to me this evening is that I think killing humans who present profound suffering or need profound care is not only an assault on that person, but one on our very selves. What I think many, including Peter, miss is that without these people calling forth love and care from us, we ourselves are diminished and hurt. I suppose like all great evils, it's masquerading as a good, a kind of cruelty clothed in false mercy, which makes it all the more difficult to unmask.[3]

Right to Life, October 22, 2020, YouTube video, https://www.youtube.com/watch?v=DB5IZXGmk08&t=856s.

[2] Singer and Connors, "Resolved: Abortion Is Immoral."

[3] E-mail sent to Stephanie Gray Connors, October 23, 2020.

This viewer's sentiment expressed my observation too. Regarding his last point about cruelty clothed in false mercy, as I prepared for my debate against Singer, one of the things I found most challenging was that he does not come across as monstrous as some of his views are, which then makes his views that are monstrous appear as not so bad.

Singer and I had a private Skype call in advance of the debate, just to get to know each other as people without discussing contentious topics, a practice I developed for my debates years ago. We discovered we had a number of things in common, including our love of travel and hiking. He is an avid surfer, and I have no doubt that my husband and he would have a smashing good time riding waves together.

When my parents watched the debate, my mom observed that Singer seemed like a friendly and calm person (his soothing Australian accent is certainly to his advantage) and someone she could have an enjoyable conversation with if she were to overlook his views on abortion and euthanasia. Moreover, Singer promotes "effective altruism," where he encourages people to share their wealth with the world's poor; in fact, Singer himself is known for doing that with significant percentages of his income.

I do not deny he has good qualities, and this is an important lesson for us who disagree with him: Singer is no different than any of us; every single one of us is a flawed human being. We all have good sides and corresponding bad sides. We all have qualities, beliefs, and behaviors worthy of emulating and those that are not. The challenge is to have the discernment to not validate the bad when someone demonstrates a good.

For example, Singer is known for propagating the drowning child thought experiment: You see a child drowning in a pond, but in order to save the child, you have to wade into the water and ruin your expensive shoes. Should you do so?[4]

The obvious answer is yes, and Singer's perspective here that we should rescue the child at personal inconvenience is a good one. On that, he and I agree. Just because he is right about that, though, does not mean he is right about abortion. In fact, I would suggest his support of abortion would be analogous to having a child and then seeing a pond and subsequently intentionally placing the child into the pond to drown. If it is wrong to leave a child to drown because you do not want to ruin your shoes when rescuing the child, it should be wrong all the more to intentionally create a situation where you drown a child.

Of course, Singer would point out that if the child is aware and would suffer, then that should stop us from drowning the child. He would then point out that since pre-born children lack the awareness and desires he deems necessary for protection, abortion is permissible.

One could certainly debate how early a human is capable of experiencing suffering (and there are studies showing some pre-born children can indeed feel pain), but

---

[4] Peter Singer, *The Life You Can Save* (New York, NY: Random House Publishing Group, 2009), 2–3.

I tend to avoid wading into specifics because that topic does not get to the heart of the matter. Instead, we need to address a more fundamental point. What about those moments when a human will not experience suffering? Is it still wrong to hurt them even if they are unaware?

In preparation for my debate against Singer, one of my mentors, Scott Klusendorf, supplied me with a great point I ended up using: Imagine you die, and someone comes to your funeral and gives a speech saying all kinds of falsehoods about you. Imagine they brutally tear down your character with one lie after another. Because you are dead, you technically are not harmed by such calumny and detraction; you are not even aware of it. You, therefore, cannot claim you have "suffered" by the person's words. And yet, wouldn't we still believe the person spreading the falsehoods did something wrong? Moreover, wouldn't we say that they wronged you by tearing down your good character and misleading others about what kind of person you had been?

Or what if someone is sleeping? What if they are in surgery and under anesthesia? In such situations, an individual is not thinking, feeling, planning, hoping, or suffering like we who read this can. Yet we would acknowledge that, by virtue of being human, they have the inherent capacity for those functions; it's just that due to their circumstances, they cannot manifest those functions in the present moment.

Human rights are not grounded in how we currently function; they are grounded in who we are. Pre-born children are human beings with the inherent capacity to behave in human ways. It's just that they cannot act on those capacities yet due to their age. As I explained once to a friend, by way of analogy, a cat has a nature to meow. It's one of their main functions. You cannot have a meow without a cat. But you can have a cat without a meow. A cat may have broken vocal cords or be sleeping and, in those states, not be able to meow, but as long as it's alive, it is still a cat even though it isn't doing what cats normally do.

The same can be said of humans: First you must have a functioner (i.e., a human) who then can manifest all types of functions (e.g., thinking, feeling pain), but sometimes they don't manifest the functions (due to age, disability, or life circumstances, such as sleeping), but as long as they are alive, then the capacity to do those functions is inherent within their nature.

Beyond that, there is another, even more fundamental point that we need to raise by drawing on the insight of Holocaust-survivor and psychiatrist Dr. Viktor Frankl, who once said, "The more one forgets himself—by giving himself to a cause to serve or another person to love—the more human he is."[5] This leads to the following question: How can one be "more" human?

Aren't you either of the species Homo sapiens or not? I think what Frankl is getting at here is, in a sense, what Singer is getting at—that there are qualities or features that go beyond the physical reality of us. Singer focuses

---

[5] Viktor Frankl, *Man's Search for Meaning* (Boston, MA: Beacon Press, 1992), 115.

a lot on whether a being is aware, has desires, or suffers (and if they demonstrate that to an adequate level in the present moment). But even a psychopath can exhibit those qualities. There are plenty of people who might, for example, test as geniuses but be morally bankrupt. That is why, when people commit homicide or genocide, we refer to these acts as "inhumane," as the actions betraying one's humanity.

If participation in evil contradicts our very nature and makes us less human, then wouldn't participation in good make us more human? Not in a physical sense but in terms of living up to our nature? In light of that, if we think about the functions Singer prioritizes, it leads us to these questions: What is our awareness for? What are our desires for? What is our thinking for? What is our consciousness for? What is our rational nature for? Our physical bodies, which have these non-physical capabilities—what are they for?

These are for love.

What good is it to be aware, rational, or intelligent if we lack love? Human beings are communal creatures. We need only look to solitary confinement as a torture technique to see the disastrous effects of isolation. Or consider orphans from Ceausescu's Romania. Or reflect on the worldwide lockdown and isolation in response to COVID-19—it led to a rise in the suicide rate, anxiety, and overall distress. We humans are made for connection, and not simply to be around each other but to have meaningful exchanges: to have communion, camaraderie, and fellowship that is grounded in love.

As Dr. Frankl also remarked, "The salvation of man is through love and in love."[6] In order to love, we need an object of love; we need another toward which we direct our affections and concern. Great movies and great stories that lift the human spirit are built around this premise.

By identifying our human nature and its capacity for love, we can then see what our bodies are for. They are the vehicles through which we live and breathe and express and receive love. They are for being in relationship with the other. We are to use our consciousness and our rational mind, even our desires, in a way that orients us to love. For any who would object, we need simply ask, "What is the alternative?" If our bodies and our ultimate purpose are not for love (and therefore for "the other"), then what are they for? The self?

Consider common airline advice given before a plane takes off. Passengers are advised that if pressure changes occur in the cabin and oxygen masks drop from the ceiling, to place one's own oxygen mask on first before helping others. Are airlines proposing selfishness? Not at all. Just the opposite, in fact. They realize that if you are not getting sufficient oxygen yourself, then as you try to help someone else, you might pass out, leaving that individual as well as yourself in danger. The airlines expect passengers will help each other out; the survival guidelines actually encourage the aid of one another—they are simply expressed in a way to ensure an individual's personal well-being too.

---

[6] Frankl, *Man's Search for Meaning*, 49.

In the Gospel of Matthew, a Pharisee asked Jesus, "Teacher, which is the great commandment in the law?" And Jesus replied, "You shall love the Lord your God with all your heart, and with all your soul, and with all your mind. This is the great and first commandment. And a second is like it, You shall love your neighbor as yourself" (Matt 22:36–39). Everything God has commanded us we can ultimately sum up in a call to love. We are souls *and* bodies. Our love for others is manifested not only in a desire for someone's good but in actual behavior that brings about another's good. It is through our bodies that we fulfill the greatest commandment; put another way, we can say our bodies are *for* love.

Someone like Singer might respond by saying that just as a newly conceived embryo cannot think or feel pain, neither can that tiny human yet love. Does that mean the littlest among us are not candidates for protection because they cannot love?

First of all, one person's inability to give love does not excuse those of us who *can* love from *being loving*. Second, in order to give love, we typically need to first receive love. This provides a template that shows us what love is. That's why motherhood and fatherhood are so important and beautiful—family life is a school of love, and parents are our first teachers. By receiving love, the maturing child learns to love. Third, since pre-born children are human, they have an inherent capacity to love; it is simply because of their young age that they have yet to develop their ability to *act* on such a capacity (which could also be said of infants).

Civil societies do not have the same expectation for the immature among us as they do for the most mature among us. We expect parents—not their toddler—to pay the bill at a restaurant. We expect teachers to keep order in their classroom—not five-year-old students. Likewise, we expect the most aware (rational, conscious) among us to use their bodies to love "the least of these" (Matt 25:45).

Saying that our bodies are for another does not give another license to take advantage of us, nor does it mean we can be forced to use our bodies in ways that go against our nature. We certainly must not confuse a free offering with a robbing.

Consider the difference between the business world promoting servant leadership versus someone being a slave. With the former, an individual is choosing to serve. With the latter, someone is being forced to submit.

Or consider the difference between a loving couple on their wedding night versus a rapist sexually assaulting someone. With the former, two parties are selflessly expressing tender love and affection for the other, but with the latter, one party is selfishly dominating and acting destructively toward another.

Or consider carrying through with a pregnancy versus having an abortion. The former communicates, "This is my body given for you," whereas the latter says, "This is your body taken for me."

This is my body given for you	*This is your body taken for me*
Servant leadership	Slavery
Loving newlyweds	Rape
Carrying a pregnancy	Abortion

Some might say that when a pre-born child uses her mother's body, that *that* is a type of slavery. Such an individual might suggest that the pre-born child is essentially non-verbally communicating to the mother, "This is your body taken for me," and that if the mother does not choose to give her body in that way, the child has no right to seize it. It is important to point out that the child did not invade the mother's body; essentially, the child is there by *invitation*.

Due to the immature nature of the youngest of our kind, pre-born children are too young to have any awareness of their own needs. Whereas a slave owner is fully aware when victimizing someone, pre-born children have no intentions whatsoever to victimize their mothers. Pre-born children are like born children: they are dependent on their mothers (fathers, or other caregivers). Civil societies expect parents to care for their dependents, not kill them. That is why parents will be charged with neglect if they refuse to feed their child who is a toddler but won't be charged with neglect if they refuse to feed their child who is a college student—the former is a dependent, and the latter is not.

Pre-born children are not choosing to enslave their mothers but instead are growing in accord with their nature in the only environment in which they should be at that stage of their development. Assuming parents raise their child well, a child will grow up to view her parents as authorities to obey, as people to honor, and as family members to love and will thus reciprocate care and compassion in the parents' old age.

How we manifest our human calling to love our neighbors should accord with our design. By nature, a woman is ordered biologically to be a mother, and motherhood, well beyond pregnancy itself, requires self-sacrifice. Moreover, a woman's uterus is designed for her offspring, so it is consistent with the usage of that organ to "give" it to one's child.

This point reminds me of the time I debated a philosophy professor at the University of Ottawa in Canada. He argued that just as a parent does not have a duty to donate her kidney to her born child who needs a transplant, a parent does not have a duty to "donate" her uterus to her pre-born child who needs a womb for nine months. The professor was certainly correct that a parent is not obligated to give away the kidney that exists in her body—but that is because the kidney is *for* her body.

There is a difference between heroism and basic obligation. The former would be extraordinary, and the latter would be ordinary. Something is ordinary when it is expected or when it is something that happens in the regular course of things. Loving others is ordinary; it is the basic expectation of human beings. But *how* we show our love for others can vary. A person might not donate her kidney to someone in need, but she might serve others in different ways. Just as our fellow human beings are temples of the Holy Spirit who are made in God's image, so are we ourselves. That is why when we are told to love our neighbors, we are told to love them *as we love ourselves.*

Someone may not pursue the extraordinary act of donating an organ due to other considerations (such as maintaining the integrity and totality of her own body in order to be physically well enough to care for her family). Having said that, there are some ways of loving others that are ordinary, and we must always fulfill them, even at personal cost or even at the cost of not serving other people. An obvious example would be meeting the needs of our offspring. This means, for example, ensuring they get enough food, clothing, shelter, and love. We could never justify denying our children those things because we feel called to leave them chained at home while we exercise to keep healthy or while we serve the poor in Africa.

Does maintaining a pregnancy fall into the category of the ordinary or the extraordinary? To answer that, we can start by looking at the uterus. If we consider its nature and purpose, we see it is an organ that, every single month, is getting ready for *someone else's body.*[7] The cyclical thickening of the uterine lining indicates

[7] Stephanie Gray, "A Kidney versus the Uterus," *Ethics and Medics*, 34, no. 10 (October 2009): 1–2, https://www.pdcnet.org/collection/fshow?id=em_2009_0034_0010_0001_0002&pdfname=em_2009_0034_0010_0001_0002.pdf&file_type=pdf.

that it is routinely preparing for the implantation of a pre-born child's body.

Consider the US National Library of Medicine's definition, which states, "The main function of the uterus is to nourish the developing fetus prior to birth."[8] The key word there is "main." While the uterus benefits a woman, its "main function" is for the needs of her child. Whereas a woman can survive without her uterus, her offspring cannot. By function, the uterus exists *more* for one's offspring than for oneself, and therefore the pre-born child can claim a right to it in a way a born child cannot claim a right to his mother's kidney.[9]

Granted, once the pre-born child exists in a woman's body, more than her uterus is involved; however, her whole body is designed for that. Her body integrates that life into a symbiotic relationship and responds in such a way as to reinforce the normalcy of a child growing in a woman's womb. In contrast, when people receive organ donations, they need to take anti-rejection drugs because their body does not expect a foreign organ within it.

It is important to admit that some women's experiences of pregnancy can be so negative that they question whether their bodies were made for it. Extreme challenges like hyperemesis gravidarum or cholestasis undoubtedly make pregnancy difficult to bear. These and other difficult conditions are not a reflection of women's bodies in general being unsuited to pregnancy; instead, they are a

[8] "Uterus," Medline Plus, last reviewed on April 1, 2023, https://medlineplus.gov/ency/imagepages/19263.htm.
[9] Gray, "A Kidney versus the Uterus."

reflection of our broken world, where disease and sickness are present. Just as some people face health challenges in a non-pregnant state, others face health challenges in a pregnant state.

Pregnancy itself, though, is a normal and expected "end" of an adult female's body. "In the beginning," before sin entered the world, our nature was designed to bring forth offspring. The very first command God gave man was to "[b]e fruitful and multiply" (Gen 1:28). And even after sin entered the world, "[b]e fruitful and multiply" (Gen 9:1) was still God's plan, as that was the command He gave to Noah and his family as well.

So if fertility, pregnancy, and motherhood are the ordinary, normal course of events, it is worth reflecting more on the symbiotic relationship between a mother and her pre-born child. Symbiosis is when two parties interact in such a way as to be mutually beneficial. In other words, pregnancy doesn't just benefit pre-born children; it benefits mothers too.

One such benefit is decreasing a woman's risk of developing breast cancer. Even the CDC acknowledges this when it says, "Having the first pregnancy after age 30, not breastfeeding, and never having a full-term pregnancy can raise breast cancer risk."[10] What is the explanation for this? Dr. Angela Lanfranchi, a surgeon who specializes in treating breast cancer, describes it well:

[10] "What Are the Risk Factors for Breast Cancer?" Centers for Disease Control and Prevention, last reviewed on July 25, 2023, https://www.cdc.gov/cancer/breast/basic_info/risk_factors.htm.

Years of published research have shed light on the breast maturation process that accounts for the protective effect of a full term pregnancy. During pregnancy breasts enlarge, doubling in volume. Due to the stimulating hormones estrogen and progesterone, the number of lobules (units of breast tissue comprised of a duct and several milk glands) increases in preparation for breast feeding. Under the influence of the pheromones hCG and hPL, made by the baby in the mother's womb, the mother's breast also matures so that cancer-vulnerable Type 1 and 2 lobules become cancer-resistant Type 3 and 4 lobules.

Most of the breast maturation needed for resistance to breast cancer does not occur, however, until after 32 weeks of pregnancy, gaining maximum protection at 40 weeks (full term). This is why a premature delivery before 32 weeks more than doubles the risk of breast cancer.[11]

Beyond the physical, a significant benefit of pregnancy to women is development of character. Of course, many things can help people grow in virtue; take, for example, playing sports or a musical instrument. These help form an individual in discipline, persistence, team work, patience, responsibility, refined concentration, and much

---

[11] Angela Lanfranchi, "Abortion and Breast Cancer: The Link That Won't Go Away," United States Conference of Catholic Bishops, accessed on September 13, 2023, https://www.usccb.org/about/pro-life-activities/respect-life-program/upload/Abortion-and-Breast-Cancer.pdf.

more. Likewise, pregnancy is a profound opportunity for growing in selflessness, surrender, discipline, patience, longanimity, love, and much more. And these are called forth from us again and again as motherhood continues post-birth. Pregnancy becomes a powerful starting point for a radical transformation of character that is not only needed to help children flourish but is actually needed to help the mother flourish.

Consider the insight of Helen Alvare. She is a lawyer, professor, associate dean, author, and speaker, but most importantly, she is a mother. She said,

> I stand before you a woman convinced that children made me, in the sense of rendering me the half-way decent person I can claim to be. . . .
>
> I REALLY had to learn that what I had initially feared—that it's not all about me and what I want to do but it's really about other people—was truer than I could ever imagine. It changed my heart in a simply-put way: I learned that life is about the other—God, my husband, my children, other people's children . . . and that that would mean everybody else. I came to be so happy about that fact, for reasons I still cannot explain. I am so incredibly happy that life is about loving others as the main thing. It means it is not a game of "how great do I need to be?" but, "how well do

I love?" And progress on that last road is sooooo good when it happens.[12]

When asked, "Has maternity affected your outlook on life, on others, on your marriage?" Helen replied,

> It has done nothing less than provide me with the path for understanding Jesus' way, the Golden Rule—the path to understanding that salvation, love, happiness, and freedom lie in learning to love. How did that hit me over the head? Just from growing in relationships with my children over the years.[13]

If our very bodies are made for love, and pregnancy is a way for women in particular to live out our purpose of love, how does abortion compare? To answer that, we need to consider what abortion does, which takes me back to a debate I participated in against a late-term abortionist.

He and I debated in front of a medical audience, where he revealed that he does abortions up to twenty-three weeks and six days. In my opening remarks, I had shown a diagram of a dilation and evacuation (D&E) abortion procedure. It was brutal. It showed a fully formed, twenty-three-weeks fetus who looked like a premature

---

[12] Sisters of Life, "Through a Mother's Eyes: What Children Teach Us (An Interview with Helen Alvare)," *Imprint*, May 2019, https://sistersoflife.org/wp-content/uploads/2019/05/SPRING-2014.pdf.
[13] Sisters of Life, "Through a Mother's Eyes."

baby, albeit in utero. The drawings showed the steps of the procedure, depicting the literal dismemberment of the child, such as an arm being pulled off and the lower body being ripped from the torso.

During cross-examination, I asked him if what I showed was an accurate representation of what he does, and he said, "It's an accurate representation." When I pressed further and said, "So it does require you pulling off of [sic] the limbs?" He responded, "It requires morcellation of, yup, morcellation is what the term is."[14]

His admission is perhaps shocking to many, but more shocking than his words are his actions. Some might respond by objecting to such a late abortion procedure while embracing earlier ones. The immorality of homicide, however, is not dependent on the age of the victim or the method of killing. It's based on the identity of the victim—is the individual a member of the human family with a right to life? If so, we need to outright reject her destruction. So whether a pre-born child is killed late in pregnancy by dismemberment or early in pregnancy by starvation, the point is that a child's life is unjustly taken from her.

Which brings us back to the theme of this chapter—what are our bodies for? Our bodies are *not* for attacking and killing our offspring. Our bodies are for love. Motherhood and fatherhood are particular identities that, by their nature, call individuals to self-sacrificing

---

[14] "Stephanie Gray vs. Dr. [Fraser] Fellows: Stephanie Gray Cross Examines Dr. Fellows," University of Western Ontario Medical School, January 2011, YouTube video, https://www.youtube.com/watch?v=tNAKPvV2YXY.

love. That love means, first and foremost, willing the good of their offspring. Protecting one's baby during pregnancy and ensuring the well-being of that same child postpartum is a physical manifestation of the beautiful and loving words "This is my body given for you."

A Post-Roe Application

When the Dobbs decision was released, the internet blew up. Famous people used social media sites like X (formerly Twitter) to decry the decision. One such person to take a public stance was former first lady Michelle Obama. She tweeted a one-page letter she wrote, generating more than seven hundred thousand likes. She made comments such as "I am heartbroken for people around this country who just lost the fundamental right to make informed decisions about their own bodies."[15] Famous singer Taylor Swift re-tweeted Obama's letter, adding her own comment: "I'm absolutely terrified that this is where we are—that after so many decades of people fighting for women's rights to their own bodies, today's decision has stripped us of that." Her post received more than eight hundred thousand likes.[16]

---

[15] Michelle Obama (@MichelleObama), "My Thoughts on the Supreme Court's Decision to Overturn Roe v. Wade," X (formerly known as Twitter), June 24, 2022, 10:46 a.m., https://twitter.com/MichelleObama/status/1540345715616006148.

[16] Taylor Swift (@taylorswift13), "I'm absolutely terrified that this is where we are," X (formerly known as Twitter), June 24, 2022, 1:14 p.m., https://twitter.com/taylorswift13/status/1540382753677627393?lang=en.

The prominence of these women and the popularity of their messages reinforces that the culture war is far from over. A new declaration from a court or a change in law does not, by itself, change the hearts of the people. There is still much work to be done to convince the public that pre-born children are worth protecting, and that convincing needs to begin with the question of what our bodies are for.

Abortion supporters like Swift and Obama all too often frame their views from the perspective of defending a woman's right to her body without ever being challenged to explain *to what end?* In other words, what are we protecting a woman's (or man's) body for? Even Christians believe our bodies are temples of the Holy Spirit and ought to be respected, that people do not have a right to inflict injustice upon another's body. That, however, does not give someone license to do just anything she wants with her own body. "Freedom," as St. John Paul II said, "consists not in doing what we like, but in having the right to do what we ought."[17]

So what ought we to do? We have a responsibility to use our bodies for the purposes for which they are designed. Man was not meant to be alone, but instead God designed us for a communion of persons where we live out a spirit of love toward God, ourselves, and one another. St. John Paul II speaks to this in *Gaudium et Spes*. He writes,

---

[17] Pope John Paul II, Homily on His Apostolic Journey to the United States (October 8, 1995), §7, https://www.vatican.va/content/john-paul-ii/en/homilies/1995/documents/hf_jp-ii_hom_19951008_baltimore.html.

God, Who has fatherly concern for everyone, has willed that all men should constitute
one family and treat one another in a spirit of
brotherhood. . . .

For this reason, love for God and neighbor is the
first and greatest commandment. Sacred Scripture,
however, teaches us that the love of God cannot
be separated from love of neighbor: "If there is
any other commandment, it is summed up in this
saying: Thou shalt love thy neighbor as thyself.
. . . Love therefore is the fulfillment of the Law"
(Rom. 13:9–10; cf. 1 John 4:20). . . .

Indeed, the Lord Jesus, when He prayed to the
Father, "that all may be one . . . as we are one"
(John 17:21–22) opened up vistas closed to human
reason, for He implied a certain likeness between
the union of the divine Persons, and the unity
of God's sons in truth and charity. This likeness
reveals that man, who is the only creature on
earth which God willed for itself, cannot fully find
himself except through a sincere gift of himself.[18]

Indeed, the woman who makes a gift of herself to her
child fully finds herself.

[18] Second Vatican Council, The Church in the Modern World
Gaudium et Spes, (December 7, 1965), §24, https://www.vatican.
va/archive/hist_councils/ii_vatican_council/documents/vat-ii_const_
19651207_gaudium-et-spes_en.html.

2

When Did Our Bodies Begin?

"What do you want to be when you grow up?" It's a question often asked of children. When I was really little, I noticed someone washing a window, and I liked how the rubber strip of the squeegee smoothly wiped away the soapy water; in that moment, I wanted to be a window washer. Let's just say my career aspirations changed as time passed, but the question asked of children isn't much different than the one commonly asked of adults.

When meeting someone new, we routinely inquire of another, "What do you do?" Both questions focus on careers, and admittedly, there's nothing wrong with that given the many hours of each day that we devote to our jobs. Although work is an important part of the human experience, we should nonetheless be cautious not to make our careers our identities. Abilities change. Jobs disappear. But we remain. And so, particularly in Catholic circles, young people are taught to discern their *vocation*, not just their careers, and they are to view such a call as more foundational than where one works for forty hours per week.

Vocation has several meanings. There is the universal vocation to love that everyone has: "God who created man out of love also calls him to love—the fundamental and innate vocation of every human being."[1] Then there is the more concrete way that we can live out the call to love, through a "Big V" vocation: marriage, priesthood, or some form of consecrated/religious life.

The vocation to marriage calls spouses first to help each other to grow in virtue to lead one another to heaven, and then to help the children they should be open to receiving, their extended family, and their community. The celibate vocations forsake the attachment to one spouse and one family in order to serve God more broadly through helping all people He directs them to, and that often goes well beyond a domestic church. Both vocation paths, married and celibate, are calls to love—one in a directed way toward one's spouse and children, the other in a more open and free way to all.

Moreover, both categories of vocation, at their heart, are actually about parenthood. Whether to marriage or a religious vocation (or even if living in a single state without a formalized "Big V" vocation), God calls all men and women, at the height of their maturity, to be spiritual fathers and mothers. As Pope Francis remarked,

> Becoming mothers and fathers really means to be fully realized, because it is to become similar to God. This is not said in the newspapers, it does

[1] CCC §1604.

not appear, but it is the truth of love. Becoming
dad and mom makes us more like God . . . You
are called to remind everyone that all the baptized,
even though in a different way, are called to be a
father or mother.[2]

We should let that sink in: we are each called to be
father or mother. Even our bodies point to this calling;
the reproductive capacity built within us tells us we were
meant to multiply, to leave a legacy of loved children.
Granted, not everyone becomes biological parents, but
we are *all* called to be spiritual parents.

The point is that we flourish and others flourish when
we live out motherhood and fatherhood. When we interact
with others by being a source of wisdom, encouragement,
counsel, nurture, comfort, protection, provision, attention, and attunement, we bless them, and we grow more
into the people God made us to be, more fully reflecting
the image of God as Father and more fully reflecting the
communion of persons and love of the Trinity.

If from our childhood adults didn't only ask us about
our career aspirations or vocation category but also asked
us to reflect on the kind of mother or father we are meant
to be, I think we could avoid a lot of problems. From
their earliest years, young people would be oriented to
think about the proper end of parenthood. This would
influence big and small decisions they make and how they

---

[2] Pope Francis, Homily of June 14, 2015, quoted by Rev. Thomas J. Olmsted,
"Into the Breach," Diocese of Phoenix, September 29, 2015, https://
dphx.org/into-the-breach/.

interact with others. It would make them spiritual parents early on, and that would not only serve them well in the present moment but also be a benefit to their future, whether they become biological parents or embrace a religious vocation.

Reflecting on our ultimate end of parenthood relates to the abortion debate in three important ways. First, with this mindset ingrained in young people, when pregnancy happens (even an unplanned one), we would be better suited to embrace the new life because we would have already been living spiritual parenthood. If we understand that we are made for parenthood, we are less likely to harm the very children God gives us to parent.

Second, God created humans for a communion of persons. Pregnancy reinforces this need whereas abortion rejects it. In other words, we cannot be mother or father if we do not have *another* to parent. Our identity as parent necessitates the very existence of someone else. And, in fact, it is that other individual whose presence changes our identity *into* parent.

Third, if, at the heights of human maturity, our identity is meant to be mother or father, then that prompts an important question: When does parenthood begin? While spiritual parenthood does not have a fixed moment per se, biological parenthood does. Since abortion relates to the latter, and if we accept that biological parenthood is a specific path of love, then we need only identify the start of parenthood to know when we should protect children's lives. In other words, parenthood (and all its duties and responsibilities) begins when a child's body begins. So when did our bodies begin?

Consider a surprise party. Guests are told to come early so they can gather and hide before the person of honor arrives. When that individual shows up and everyone yells "Surprise!" or "Happy Birthday!" she finally becomes aware that people had congregated for her. But their existence in her home occurred *before* her knowledge of it. In other words, they didn't appear in her house when she arrived; rather, they appeared earlier.

So it is with pre-born children. Their presence pre-dates a mother's knowledge of it. At the very beginnings of a pre-born child's life, he is hidden like the guests at a surprise party. When a woman takes a pregnancy test and it is positive, the test tells her *that* a pre-born child is present, but it does not tell her *when* the child became present (and therefore when her biological motherhood began). If the test is merely an announcement or declaration of a fact, at what point *before* the test did the child come to be?

Some would say the answer to that question is inconclusive. That there is much debate. Many opinions. No clear answer. Such responses, however, overlook that science has, in fact, given us an unambiguous answer. Basic biology teaches that animals that reproduce sexually (a category that includes humans) begin their lives at fertilization, otherwise known as sperm-egg fusion.

Consider the opening paragraph of a prominent medical textbook, *The Developing Human*. It says, "Human development is a continuous process that begins when an oocyte (ovum) from a female is fertilized by a sperm (spermatozoon) from a male."[3] This acknowledges two important facts: (1) humans are always developing ("continuous") and (2) that development's starting point is sperm-egg fusion.

This point is again emphasized in the book in Chapter 2, where it says, "Human development begins at fertilization when a sperm fuses with an oocyte to form a single cell, the zygote. This highly specialized, *totipotent cell* (capable of giving rise to any cell type) marks the beginning of us as a unique individual."[4] That is presented as fact, not theory. It is clear and concise. And it is what our future physicians are given to read in medical school.

Even when such a miniscule body is only one cell, it contains DNA that is different from that of the mother and father. The DNA that distinguishes each of us today was determined back then.

It is worth pointing out, though, that the embryo with that distinct DNA is different from, say, a skin cell that also has that DNA. My skin cells have my DNA, but they are a *part* of me. When I was newly conceived as an embryo, that cell was *entirely* me. No one need fear that a shedding skin cell will suddenly become a new person. But at sperm-egg fusion, that one-celled embryo *is* a new person. If you put a skin cell in the exact environment an embryo is in, the skin cell will not move through the

[3]   Keith L. Moore, T. V. N. Persaud, and Mark G. Torchia, *The Developing Human: Clinically Oriented Embryology* (Philadelphia, PA: Elsevier, 2016), 1.

[4]   Moore, Persaud, and Torchia, *The Developing Human*, 11.

stages of human development on a trajectory toward adulthood like an embryo will.

Put another way, the embryo doesn't grow into a person but instead *is* a person who grows into an older version of herself (or himself). After sperm-egg fusion, we simply need time to grow and develop. Our individual identity remains the same even as our bodies and minds mature, both before and after birth. Some might say we don't *look* very human when our bodies are only one cell, but that's actually false. We look exactly as a human should look at that stage of human development.

Our bodies do not begin as a sperm, for if the sperm that had half of our DNA fertilized a different egg than the one that contributed to us, we would not exist. Likewise, if the egg that had half our DNA was fertilized by a sperm different than the one that contributed to us, we would not exist. Sperm and egg are parts of our father and mother, respectively, but alone they are not us. Yes, they *contributed* to who we are, but it was their union that was necessary for our bodies to come to be. Once that union occurs, we come into existence.

After all, consider yourself today. Obviously you didn't come into existence when you woke up this morning. What about the day before? A month before today? Two months ago? A year ago? What about when you were five? An infant? We can all agree that you were you the whole time even though your body was smaller and less developed when you were younger compared to now. What about the day before your mom gave birth? Was the baby that was you at birth also you the day before? What about two days before? A month?

The point of these questions is to get us thinking about the most logical place to draw the line for our beginning. Working backwards from where we are today to where we began, the most logical starting point is sperm-egg fusion. Any point after that will be arbitrary, based on a degree of development rather than on the moment of existence.

Having said that, someone who has studied biology might raise the subject of identical twins, of which my mom is one. My mom and my Aunt Corinne came from the union of one sperm and one egg (in contrast to fraternal twins, of which my mother-in-law is one, where two eggs are released in ovulation and two different sperm fertilize them). So either my mom *or* my aunt began her life at fertilization—we don't know who—and in the days following, but prior to implantation, that one individual split into two, and so came to be the identical twin. This means, in such very rare circumstances, someone can come to be *after* fertilization; however, the fact that anomalies happen does not negate what is the norm. Moreover, one individual still had to come into existence at fertilization in order for the identical twin to follow.

This can happen with other species too. Take a flatworm—if you cut one in half, you will get two flatworms. The fact that one flatworm, or one human, has an incredible ability to split into two does not mean there was no individual prior to the split.

From a biological perspective, we can reasonably say that the living body of a new individual offspring that is different from an adult male and female comes into existence at sperm-egg fusion. We can also reasonably say that this is how the vast majority of us began our lives. We can further reasonably say that a miniscule number of us, those who are identical twins, began their lives by suddenly splitting off from someone who came into existence at fertilization.

After fertilization has occurred, a singleton simply develops more, but he does not take on a new identity. He is the same individual at fertilization as he is at three days, three weeks, three months, and birth. Granted, his appearances and abilities change dramatically during pregnancy, but that is no different than his appearances and abilities changing dramatically between birth and adulthood. Similarly, after twinning has occurred, a twin simply develops more but does not take on a new identity.

If this is true, why do people claim there is a debate about when life begins? I would suggest it is because they are confusing a biological question about when the body begins with a philosophical one about how we ought to treat the body after it comes into being.

The pro-life position is that where there is a living body of a member of the human family, we ought to treat that individual with respect, regardless of her age. Any alternative position that says that we ought to protect only some members of the human family is not grounded in science; instead, it is grounded in an idea that not all humans are equal.

It is worth pointing out that the bodies of the youngest of our kind develop remarkably early in utero. By eight to ten weeks of pregnancy, female embryos already have ovaries,[5] and when they reach twenty weeks, they have on average between six and seven million eggs.[6] Ironically abortion is often justified on the basis of women's rights while completely overlooking the rights of females in the womb.

That pro-lifers embrace the fact that life begins at fertilization is sometimes met with disbelief from abortion supporters. They question whether the pro-lifer really embraces that view in practice. A supposed test of this came several years ago when a thought experiment made its way around the internet. It went something like this: Imagine there is a burning building with one hundred frozen embryos and a two-year-old in it. You can run out of the building with *either* the one hundred frozen embryos *or* the two-year-old, but not both. Whom do you pick?

The dilemma is presented expecting that most, if not everyone, would save the toddler, thereby calling into question the pro-life belief that pre-born children are just as human as toddlers. Does it follow that if you choose the toddler instead of the embryos that the embryos are subhuman and less valuable?

---

[5] "Prenatal Summary," Endowment for Human Development, accessed on September 14, 2023, https://www.ehd.org/prenatal-summary.php.

[6] "How Many Eggs Does a Woman Have?" Medical News Today, last updated on February 13, 2023, https://www.medicalnewstoday.com/articles/how-many-eggs-does-a-woman-have#early-years.

To answer that, consider this variation of the thought experiment: Imagine there is a burning building with two newborns and your own baby in it. You can run out of the building with *either* the two infants *or* your own baby, but not all three. Whom do you pick? If a parent picks saving her own child over the children she does not know, the other children are still valuable humans.

The choice simply shows that we tend to prioritize those with whom we have emotional connections and familial relationships. Similarly with the frozen embryos versus toddler scenario, someone may choose the toddler because they have a relationship with her. Or someone may choose the toddler because they believe the born child is more likely to survive after removal from the building than the embryos are. But choosing the toddler does not mean the embryos are subhuman. Ultimately all parties are human and have a right to life, but sadly, sometimes we cannot save everyone. That doesn't mean we may directly kill those we cannot save.

The burning building scenario could be summarized as "Two people (or groups of people) are dying. Whom do we save?" In contrast, pregnancy could be summarized as "Two people are living. May we intentionally kill the younger of the two?" The reality is, the younger one is still human—just less developed. She or he began life at fertilization and therefore ought not be harmed. To believe in human equality is to acknowledge that by virtue of their membership in the human family, we should protect and respect the youngest of our kind like we do for those who are older.

Pre-born children undoubtedly have much development and maturation to do, but so do infants and other young children. Our developmental level might be important for some rights, like voting, but it is not relevant for other rights, like the right to life. Given that human embryos and fetuses are children as we all once were, they should be given the chance to grow up to be the parents we all are meant to be. Since motherhood and fatherhood are our ultimate destinies, we should reverence the very individuals whose existence bestows on us those grand titles.

A Post-Roe Application

Since the overturning of Roe, one of the most contentious debates involves medical abortion. This method ends pre-born lives via medicine instead of surgery. The woman herself administers the abortion, and it is intended to be done early in pregnancy. Typically it involves taking two types of drugs: mifepristone and misoprostol. Mifepristone blocks the hormone progesterone, which is needed for a pregnancy to successfully develop (think "pro-gestate").

Twenty-four to forty-eight hours after taking mifepristone, a woman takes misoprostol to cause contractions, and then she begins to bleed, expelling the baby and related pregnancy tissue. The Guttmacher Institute reports that more than half of all abortions in America are now via pill instead of surgery.[7]

---

[7] Rachel K. Jones et al., "Medication Abortion Now Accounts for More Than Half of All US Abortions," Guttmacher Institute, February 24, 2022,

In states where abortion is banned, there is an effort to make abortion accessible for women without having them travel to a neighboring state, and a way of doing that is by using telemedicine for a woman to get approval for pills that are then mailed to her home. But a legal battle is currently raging around this. Pro-life groups are suing the FDA for its approval of abortion pills, and with the case having gone through the court of appeals, it is now expected to be heard by the Supreme Court— and pro-lifers are hoping for another positive decision like Dobbs.

But even if we can curtail the provision of abortion pills coming from American physicians in states favorable to abortion access, there are already international work-arounds. There are groups in Europe, Mexico, and India, for example, that have elaborate networks to get abortion pills to women in the United States. Some women within the United States even have pill packing parties in their homes and then deliver them to women they meet online. One website of an international initiative even recommends that women order abortion pills in advance of becoming pregnant—just so they have a stock at home *in case* they need it in order to avoid international mailing delays if they want to abort at a future point.

The abortion pill underworld is profoundly sinister. Some women are accepting pills from strangers with no way of ensuring that they are the actual medication

https://www.guttmacher.org/article/2022/02/medication-abortion-now-accounts-more-half-all-us-abortions.

or that they aren't laced with a substance such as fentanyl. Some distributors of abortion pills even promote "self-managed abortion," where women take the medicine without proper, if any, oversight from a medical professional. It has led to women taking the pills much later in pregnancy (some sites even advertising up to thirteen weeks), which is well beyond the seven-week cutoff the FDA first approved for mifepristone in 2000 (before extending it to ten weeks in 2016).

One particularly dark aspect of abortion pills is that they mimic a miscarriage. (Some pro-abortion websites even advise women who experience complications from abortion pills to falsely claim that they think they're having a miscarriage when presenting at an emergency room in order to avoid possible criminal charges in states where abortion is illegal.) Abortion pills are a devious counterfeit of miscarriage. The latter is a tragedy, where the baby dies through no one's fault; the former is a moral evil because the child is living and then someone intentionally inflicts death upon him. And yet, we can learn from the realities of miscarriage how risky the pursuit of abortion pills can be.

In my own experience of four miscarriages, the bleeding is brutal. I miscarried each time without medical or surgical intervention, but it was not easy. Medical professionals watched me very closely. It wasn't entirely an "at home" experience, because on several occasions, I was either going to the doctor's office, the hospital, or laboratories. I had countless ultrasounds to ensure I did not have an ectopic pregnancy and to check, once I started passing tissue, whether all the tissue had left my body.

On several occasions, I had retained tissue, and doctors monitored me very closely with more ultrasounds, medical appointments, and bloodwork in the days following to make sure my body was completing the miscarriage and that I was not developing an infection. Related to that, my medical team regularly tested my blood, looking at my white blood cell count to check my immunity, my hemoglobin levels to ensure my body could handle more blood loss, and my HCG levels to ensure they were dropping in accord with the end of a pregnancy.

Generally my husband was able to be home with me, and when he wasn't, I had friends come over. Several times my blood loss was so rapid that we feared I was on the cusp of hemorrhaging.

I therefore find it very troubling when I read online promotions of the abortion pill that portray it as a minor and easy experience that does not require all the monitoring I had in my miscarriages. That women, especially teenagers or those trying to hide their pregnancies, would secretly take drugs without proper supervision and examination puts them at risk for infection, hemorrhage, and other health complications.

Of course, one could make the point that choosing to inflict homicide on one's child brings with it natural risks to oneself. A woman could avoid all the harms of abortion to herself by avoiding abortion entirely. As the abortion pill debate heats up, it is worth highlighting risks to women's health, as well as two more points as they relate to this chapter's theme.

The abortion pill is a direct attack on the nature of motherhood. Mothers of newborns worry if they aren't producing enough breastmilk. When there was a formula shortage, people worried that they would not be able to provide adequate nutrition for their babies. Even mothers of adult children typically love making food and providing their children with leftovers and freezer meals. It is within a mother's nature to provide and sustain. Abortion pills may *seem* innocuous because a woman takes them early, when she may not yet discern a baby or feel her child kick. But on deeper examination, they are heinous—because they take the child's safe and nurturing environment and make it hostile, leading to the child's starvation and expulsion.

Consider news stories that show pictures of children who are malnourished in poor countries or who were held captive in conditions of squalor. We are rightly horrified when precious humans are denied their basic needs. That a medical abortion does not dismember or decapitate like a surgical one does not make it any better. It still deprives the youngest of our kind the necessities of life and does so by the hand of the mother who is entrusted to love—not harm.

Second, if a pre-born child's body does not begin at fertilization, and if an early embryo is not a separate human being from the mother, why would there be a need for the early intervention of abortion pills? If the embryo is nothing, then surely no action would be needed.

The fact that a woman takes pills to terminate (i.e., *end*) a pregnancy is an admission that the child's body had already *begun*.

When abortion supporters promote early abortion, it can sometimes feel like a challenge for pro-lifers to adequately rebut because the baby is so underdeveloped. But on the contrary, pro-lifers can view discussions about early abortion as important opportunities to raise the question of whose body the abortion pills are ultimately targeting and how that body began at fertilization.

3

When Our Bodies Become Home

The summer of 2022 was another exceptionally hot and dry one for the state of California. Fires were raging in and near Yosemite National Park that July, and while my husband and I were vacationing in the Pacific Northwest, he received a call from his brother. In shock, he relayed to me matter-of-factly, "My parents' home just burned down."

We were devastated. It was a home my husband, his siblings, and their father had built with their own hands, slowly over years. The house was so custom-built that it featured a geodesic dome along with a stone and mortar basement, using stones that they quarried from the property. The manual labor was intense and took great skill, genius, and patience. When we scoured the internet for news stories that night, we saw an aerial view of the fire with the newscaster saying, "It appears there is a structure engulfed in flames."

"Oh my gosh," my husband said. "That's my parents' house!" He played and replayed the footage. What we knew in our minds was now visually burned into our hearts. And time would indeed confirm that the fire had blackened their twenty acres of land. The house was entirely gone. We would also come to learn the fire spread so rapidly that my in-laws hadn't received an evacuation phone call. They only knew to leave because they looked out a window and saw flames surrounding their home. The soles of my mother-in-law's shoes were burned in her escape. They barely made it out alive.

Home. It means so much to human beings. It is the place where we make countless memories. A physical structure takes on a new identity when we associate it with our formative years as children. A building becomes a sign of belonging, comfort, and camaraderie. Amidst the tragedy of the loss of my in-laws' homestead, though, was the consolation that we did not lose our loved ones. Home, at its heart, is special because of the people with whom we share or shared it. In fact, one might refer to being with another person as being at home.

That brings to mind an article I wrote a few months before the fire. I reflected,

> Our first lesson that home is ultimately a person more than a place is taught to us by the youngest of our kind.
>
> Pre-born children do not know the sights, sounds, and smells of man-made architecture. Instead, home for them is the person of their mother. It is the sound of her heartbeat and voice. It is the warmth and comfort of her womb. That is why, when a baby is newly born, placing the crying child on the chest of her mother

instantly soothes. Because in that moment, the child is home.[1]

Those who favor abortion might object to my referencing a woman as being "home" for her pre-born child. They might mistakenly conclude that since a home is an object, I am turning women into objects by my statement. They might claim that the pro-life movement views women as "incubators" and wants to deny women freedom, creating a world akin to *The Handmaid's Tale*. That novel by my fellow Canadian author Margaret Atwood (and the related television series by the same name) is a futuristic story. It imagines a world where most women are unable to reproduce, so a group of fertile women—the handmaids—are forced to have sex with men whose wives cannot conceive with them. Women are raped. They are denied basic freedoms. They are treated as slaves.

The idea that being anti-abortion makes one akin to the weird world of *The Handmaid's Tale* is as twisted as the dystopian storyline itself. And yet, this notion is so widespread that in the spring of 2022, it was common for abortion advocates to dress up in the red cape and white bonnet of the handmaids when protesting the US Supreme Court's reversal of Roe v. Wade. Some people actually believe pro-lifers are bringing a fictional world to life.

In reality, a pro-life world is the opposite of Atwood's "Republic of Gilead," where brutal injustice takes place.

[1] Stephanie Gray Connors, "When Home Is a Person, Not a Place," *Catholic Answers*, January 24, 2022, https://www.catholic.com/magazine/online-edition/when-home-is-a-person-not-a-place.

The pro-life movement never supports rape. Nor does it support enlisting someone outside of one's marriage to have sex with a married man. It does not support rounding women up and forcing them to gestate other peoples' children.

Instead, the pro-life movement believes in the love between a mother and her child. It believes parents have a responsibility to meet the needs of their children. And it believes the beautiful relationship of family is what ultimately roots people, making "home" the person or people of one's kin. That is why my husband can still experience the beauty of home when visiting his parents and siblings even though the structure they built is no more.

Put that way, it should not be controversial to refer to a pregnant woman as "home" for her pre-born child. As a woman who is a mother, I would say such a notion is beautiful. And yet, when the US Supreme Court released its Dobbs decision, I saw a news story that featured abortion supporters holding signs that said, "Women are not incubators."

I'll never forget the day I got special access to a neonatal intensive care unit with rows of incubators. A nurse friend of mine was charged with caring for these tiniest of babies who should still have been in wombs but for whom, due to various circumstances, birth came early. I washed up and then walked between the smallest humans I'd ever seen, who were residing in little "homes" that were keeping them alive.

One baby girl was only a day out of the womb at twenty-six weeks, and while she had a full head of thick, black hair, her miniscule size left me in wonder that such a baby was still alive. I was in awe of the skilled people, like my friend, who ministered so devotedly to these vulnerable infants, successfully preserving the lives of so many of them.

Are women like the incubators on my friend's hospital ward? An incubator is "an apparatus with a chamber used to provide controlled environmental conditions especially for the cultivation of microorganisms or the care and protection of premature or sick babies."[2]

While a woman most certainly is not an apparatus, notice the words "cultivation," "care," and "protection." What woman wouldn't want to be known for cultivating, caring, and protecting? Indeed, ask a mother at the bedside of her pre-term infant, whose fragile skin is not ready for the outside world and who has various cords attached to him with various devices monitoring him, "Would you rather your baby be able to spend this time in your womb instead of the incubator?" and you will get a resounding "Yes!" An incubator is a last resort. It is something that is bittersweet; it is celebrated as a means to save her child's life, but it is also a less-than-ideal environment that places a barrier between the mother and her child. Such a mother would happily return to doing what an incubator does.

Of course, saying that does not demean the mother, nor does it make her a machine. It simply acknowledges

---

[2] *Merriam-Webster*, s.v. "incubator," accessed September 14, 2023, https://www.merriam-webster.com/dictionary/incubator.

that mothers instinctively want to do what they can to "cultivate," "care," and "protect" their children's lives.

As with many words, though, the term incubator has multiple definitions. In fact, I was struck by this alternative one: "an organization or place that aids the development of new business ventures especially by providing low-cost commercial space, management assistance, or shared services."[3] Again, why object to being an incubator if that is the definition? Isn't aiding the development of something, providing a step up for something that is having a difficult time making it, a role we celebrate? So if it's nice for an organization to be an incubator for another organization, all the more isn't it nice for a human to be an incubator for another human, particularly when the humans involved are a mother and her vulnerable child?

Perhaps abortion supporters aren't viewing an incubator like the above but instead are thinking about it more from this third definition: "an apparatus by which eggs are hatched artificially."[4] That conjures up images of chickens, of an assembly line, of manufacturing, and of unnatural quantities.

Is that what pregnancy is though? Hardly. No one in the pro-life movement is suggesting viewing women like that. As mentioned earlier, no one in the pro-life movement is suggesting lining up women to have random babies mechanistically inserted into them.[5] No one in

---

[3] *Merriam-Webster*, s.v. "incubator."

[4] *Merriam-Webster*, s.v. "incubator."

[5] I've previously published my objections to IVF and surrogacy through my book *Conceived by Science: Thinking Carefully and Compassionately about Infertility and IVF.*

the pro-life movement is suggesting viewing women as objects. Instead, we are suggesting that when a woman's own flesh and blood naturally come into existence as her child in her body, that she be faithful to the needs of the person who is the fruit of her womb.

So while a pregnant woman is not a machine, she is a mother, and her female body is perfectly suited to provide the environment her pre-born child needs for care and protection; from this perspective, she is an "incubator."

Having said that, I think even better terms to describe the beauty of pregnancy and the home of her body that a woman gives to her child would be *"sanctuary"* or *"tabernacle."*

These words connote the sacred, the set apart, and the holy. Something that is sacred elicits our reverence. We treat it with care, awe, and wonder. We set it apart as special, as something extraordinary.

In Jewish tradition, a tabernacle was the dwelling place of God. Catholic tradition maintains that notion by using tabernacles to hold the Eucharist—the Body of Christ. And that means a tabernacle once took on living form, more than two thousand years ago, in the identity of a pregnant Jewish teenager, Mary of Nazareth. It was her very womb that became the dwelling place for God made flesh, for the Incarnation. It was she who became a walking tabernacle, visiting her pregnant cousin Elizabeth, who acknowledged the sacred within Mary by declaring, "Blessed are you among women, and *blessed is the fruit of your womb*!" (Luke 1:42, emphasis added).

Every woman who bears a child carries within her a life made in God's image, and therefore, she bears semblance to a tabernacle. I found myself meditating on this reality in a small adoration chapel in Vancouver, Canada.

During a visit to relatives, my husband, daughter, and I stopped at the parish where a dear priest friend of mine is pastor. As we knelt before an ornate, gold-covered, jewel-bedecked tabernacle, I stared through its window, which revealed, by all appearances, a white host of bread, but which, by substance, had been transformed into the Body of Christ. As it should happen, I was newly pregnant, my pre-born child only a few weeks old.

There I was, face-to-face, with the power of the sacred, the beauty of the tabernacle made of such riches as a way to honor what—*whom*—it contained. And as God was mysteriously small and hidden, I thought about how my pre-born child was too. The tabernacle was grand precisely to point us to the majesty of who dwelt within. And I realized that wasn't only the case for the gold box. It was also the case for me. I was to be treated with reverence and respect, not only because I myself am made in God's image, but because, most particularly in that season of pregnancy, I bore within my body new life made in the image of the Divine.

A tabernacle points to the grandness of God, hidden in the host, and a pregnant woman points to the dignity of pre-born life, hidden in the underdeveloped embryo and fetus. Women have a sacred power, by virtue of our femininity, to conceive and bear new life. Venerable

Joseph Cardinal Mindszenty acknowledged as much when he wrote,

> The most important person on earth is a mother. She cannot claim the honor of having built Notre Dame Cathedral. She need not. She has built something more magnificent than any cathedral—a dwelling for an immortal soul, the tiny perfection of her baby's body. . . . The Angels have not been blessed with such a grace. They cannot share in God's creative miracle to bring new saints to Heaven. Only a human mother can. Mothers are closer to God the Creator than any other creatures; God joins forces with mothers in performing this act of creation. . . . What on God's good earth is more glorious than this: To be a mother?[6]

Celebrating the heights of greatness to which motherhood lifts a woman does not mean motherhood is easy—whether before or after birth. One can see beauty in a particular state of life while acknowledging hardships in it too. In fact, in December 2020, I sent this text to a couple of friends: "Being a wife is easy," I wrote. "Being a mom is hard."

Around the seventh week of my pregnancy with Violet, "morning" sickness hit (which was not limited to the

---

[6] Cardinal Joseph Mindszenty, "Mother," EWTN, accessed on September 14, 2023, https://www.ewtn.com/catholicism/library/mother-11253.

hours around dawn). For the next six weeks, I found myself frequently passed out on the couch or on our bed. It wasn't just exhaustion. I felt gross. Really gross. My body was transforming before my eyes, and it did not feel pleasant. Sleep gave only temporary relief, and I'd often wake up feeling worse than when I first lay down. Things I once loved, like reading, I couldn't fathom doing. It was as though a dark cloud was hanging over me.

Constantly feeling sick affected me physically and emotionally. I remember sobbing to my husband one afternoon when I felt particularly miserable. I expressed that I felt bad that I wasn't doing things around the house, like cooking and cleaning (stuff I had happily done before), and that my husband was carrying a heavier load as a result. And then he reminded me that I was growing another human being inside me. As I was oriented outward to help our child, he pointed out, he would be oriented outward to help me.

Although I experienced the welcome relief of the second trimester "glow," some women face pregnancy sickness that is longer and more intense. A friend of mine, for example, experienced hyperemesis gravidarum during her pregnancy, which is extreme and persistent nausea and vomiting. For her, that led to regular visits to the hospital, where she received IV fluids. Or I think of my sister, who felt sick and exhausted with her pregnancy but had four other children to take care of!

Regardless of one's degree of sickness or tiredness during some or all of pregnancy, the very reality of having another human being in your body is a tangible reminder that our lives are not our own. That perspective might be offensive to some in our self-absorbed culture, but I look at it as a beautiful sign that we were made to love. The pregnant woman is constantly encouraged to orient her mindset outside of herself to the one who is within herself: from foods she shouldn't eat, to activities she shouldn't do, to optimal sleeping positions, to staying healthy and strong—all of these are for the well-being of her growing child.

Mothers are incredible at living a life of sacrifice. I think of my own mom and how much she put my sister and me ahead of herself. If there was a favorite dessert left over, she'd give it to us and not take a piece for herself. She would take us shopping for new outfits, but because money was tight, she rarely, if ever, seemed to shop for herself. When we were sick, she would get up in the night and help us. Her life and comforts were constantly interrupted in order to serve and bless her children.

When a mother lives out "This is my body given for you," it is so much more than welcoming her offspring into her womb. It is the totality of her person—arms to hold, breasts to feed, hands to clean, mouth to sing, and mind to teach; in other words, a heart to love and a whole body with which to serve day after day, month after month, year after year.

Several years ago when I was at Florida State University displaying a pro-life exhibit, I debated with a crowd of students. Eventually people in the crowd began conversing with each other, and I didn't have to say anything. I marveled at one pro-life student in the group who looked at an abortion-supporter and asked him why he needed a mother. He replied, "To take care of me and make sure I didn't get hurt." The pro-lifer responded, "Exactly. Mothers are supposed to take care of their children."

Mothers naturally care for their young, so it shouldn't surprise us that when God wants to convey how much He loves us, He uses references to mothers and their children. Isaiah 49:15 says, "Can a woman forget her nursing child, or show no compassion for the child of her womb? Even these may forget, yet I will not forget you" (NRSV).

Or consider St. Paul's words in his First Letter to the Thessalonians: "Just as a nursing mother cares for her children, so we cared for you. Because we loved you so much, we were delighted to share with you not only the gospel of God but our lives as well" (1 Thess 2: 7–8, NIV).

Or consider Jesus's own words when He laments the poor example of religious leadership and the failure of teachers to properly lead. He says, "O Jerusalem, Jerusalem, killing the prophets and stoning those who are sent to you! How often would I have gathered your children together as a hen gathers her brood under her wings, and you would not!" (Matt 23:37). The image Jesus uses of a hen gathering her chicks is very powerful. Consider this reflection:

> The Renaissance writer Ulisse Aldrovandi described how, at the first sign of a predator, mother hens will immediately gather their chicks "under the shadow of their wings, and with this

covering they put up such a very fierce defense—striking fear into their opponent in the midst of a frightful clamor, using both wings and beak—they would rather die for their chicks than seek safety in flight." Similarly, in collecting food, the mother hen allows her chicks to eat their fill before satisfying her own hunger. Thus, he said, mother hens present, in every way, "a noble example of love for their offspring."[7]

We see that in other animals too. Around the time of my debate against Peter Singer, I came across a news story of a viral video I ended up incorporating into my remarks. It was about a runner in Utah who was stalked by a cougar for six minutes and feared he would be mauled to death. Why did the cougar follow and threaten the runner for so long? Because the runner had been approaching the cougar's two babies, and that momma cougar thought he was a threat to her children. The cougar mother is a great witness for human mothers. By her actions, her message was to protect our offspring.

In contrast to the ugly world in *The Handmaid's Tale* is the beautiful world in *The Lord of the Rings*. In that epic adventure, a young hobbit named Frodo is tasked with saving civilization from evil and destruction. At one

---

[7] Karen Davis, "The Hen Is a Symbol of Motherhood for Reasons We May Have Forgotten, So Let Us Recall," United Poultry Concerns, May 11, 2023, https://www.upc-online.org/alerts/180512_the_hen_is_symbol_of_motherhood.html#:~:text=The%20Renaissance%20writer%20Ulisse%20Aldrovandi,a%20frightful%20clamor%2C%20using%20both.

point in the story, between moments of great hardship and strife, Frodo and his friends make it to a place of refuge. The book describes it as follows:

> Frodo was now safe in the Last Homely House east of the Sea. That house was, as Bilbo had long ago reported, "a perfect house, whether you like food or sleep, or story-telling or singing, or just sitting and thinking best, or a pleasant mixture of them all." Merely to be there was a cure for weariness, fear and sadness.[8]

That beautiful description is what a woman gets to be for her pre-born child. In her very person, by her very presence, she gets the privilege of being "a cure for weariness, fear and sadness." In a word, she gets to be *home*.

A Post-Roe Application

Around the time of the Dobbs decision, Florida was one state that cut back on abortion access—first down to fifteen weeks and then down to six weeks. The *Washington Post* featured a story about a pregnant woman at odds with the state's law.[9] When she was twenty-three weeks

---

[8]   J. R. R. Tolkien, *The Lord of the Rings: The Fellowship of the Ring* (London: Grafton, 1992), 241.

[9]   This story was featured in these articles: Frances Stead Sellers, "Her Baby Has a Deadly Diagnosis. Her Florida Doctors Refused an Abortion," *Washington Post*, February 18, 2023, https://www.washingtonpost.com/health/2023/02/18/florida-abortion-ban-unviable-pregnancy-potter-syndrome/; Frances Stead Sellers, Thomas Simonetti, and Maggie Penman,

along, an ultrasound revealed there were problems with her baby's development, and she learned that her child had Potter Syndrome. The kidneys of such babies don't develop properly, if at all. Without properly functioning kidneys, there is insufficient amniotic fluid, which then impacts lung development and creates a cascade of other problems.

It was traditionally understood that such babies would die at, or shortly after, birth. Recent medical advancements, however, are starting to change this. For example, Jaime Herrera Beutler, a former congresswoman, was told her baby had Potter Syndrome and that it was 100 percent fatal, but she pursued an experimental treatment of amnioinfusions to replace the missing amniotic fluid. Her daughter was born without kidneys and ultimately received a kidney donation from her father. Today she is ten years old.[10]

In the case of the Florida couple, their baby had no kidneys and a doctor told them their child's condition was "incompatible with life."[11] They wanted to end the pregnancy shortly after learning this, but the doctors were concerned that the new state abortion law would not allow them to perform an abortion. Although this couple ultimately gave birth at thirty-seven weeks (their

"The Short Life of Baby Milo," *Washington Post*, May 19, 2023, https://www.washingtonpost.com/health/interactive/2023/florida-abortion-law-deborah-dorbert/?itid=hp-top-table-main_p001_f004&itid=lk_interstitial_manual_8.

[10] Dana Bash, "How Rep. Herrera Beutler Saved Her Baby," CNN, August 9, 2017, https://www.cnn.com/2017/06/12/politics/jaime-herrera-beutler-badass-women-of-washington/index.html.

[11] Sellers, "Her Baby Has a Deadly Diagnosis."

son died ninety-nine minutes after birth), they went public conveying their outrage that they couldn't terminate the pregnancy in their state when they wanted to.

When we come from the perspective that a pregnant woman gets the privilege of being *home* for her child, this woman's attitude is very sad. If a pre-born child has a fatal condition, that reality should compel parents to embrace the fullness of pregnancy even more—for it is only in pregnancy that their child will experience the majority, or the entirety, of life.

Consider that when an adult has a terminal illness and is given the choice between dying at home or in a clinical environment, "home" is typically the preferred choice. People want to depart this earth surrounded by loved ones in the atmosphere and place that most brings them peace, happy memories, comfort, and familiarity. For a pre-born child who will die at or shortly after birth, his or her mother is that home. Even amidst profound heartache, the simple truth is that mothers should not evict their sick pre-born children just because they are going to have incredibly short lives.

This perspective isn't meant to minimize the profound suffering of mothers in these types of situations and the understandable emotional upheaval they endure when learning their baby will die shortly after birth. There is no denying the pain that will come when strangers notice one's pregnant belly and excitedly ask about the expected child, only to find herself explaining she's preparing for a birth *and a* funeral.

Rather than pursuing "termination" in these heart-breaking situations, we need people to guide us to do the right thing even when it's hard, to help us see with different eyes, to change our perspective if a situation cannot be changed, and to embrace the privilege of being the only home one's child may ever know. The short season of sheltering one's sick baby beneath the mother's heart can become a sacred time to bond with her child and to allow for proper closure when the child eventually passes. This is why perinatal hospice is a bright alternative to pursuing abortion.

Dr. Byron Calhoun is one of the pioneers of perinatal hospice. In a beautiful essay in which he explained its philosophy, he wrote,

> We employed the seminal concepts of Kubler-Ross on modern medicine's understanding of death and dying to aid us in shaping our care model. While Kubler-Ross transformed the discussions around death, Saunders revolutionized the care of the dying with her modern hospice movement. The unifying concept in hospice remains the holistic approach to the physical, emotional, and spiritual support for dying patients and their families. The core belief in hospice is to offer treatment of the dying that respects their dignity and *sees them as truly alive and not yet dead* [emphasis added]. . . .
>
> Perinatal hospice families who choose to carry their pregnancies in which the fetus has a lethal

condition possess many of the same characteristics of families with a terminally ill adult or
child, a clinical scenario in which hospice has
been well accepted and a useful method of care.
Many of the hospice principles were successfully
applied in perinatal hospice. The emphasis is
on affirming life by care for the loved one, yet
regarding dying as a normal part of life. A conscious effort is made to neither hasten death nor
prolong dying. The team stresses values beyond
the mere physical needs of the dying individual
and *allows the parents to "parent" their child*
[emphasis added] for whatever time they are
allowed. The family is supported in their medical, emotional, and spiritual needs through an
organized, multidisciplinary team that cares for
them after the death of the loved child during
the period of grief.

The care in perinatal hospice differs in emphasis, but not in type of care from other modes of
perinatal care. Its primary focus is on the family—
not the fetal diagnosis and attendant anomalies.
The family is placed in the center of the care and
there is a continuum of support from the diagnosis, through death, and grief. As Amy Kuebelbeck,
author of *Waiting with Gabriel*, a book about her
own experience with her son who had a fatal form
of hypoplastic left heart, notes, "I know that some
people assume that continuing a pregnancy with
a baby who will die is all for nothing. But it isn't

all for nothing. *Parents can wait with their baby, protect their baby, and love their baby for as long as that baby is able to live* [emphasis added]. They can give that baby a peaceful life—and a peaceful goodbye. That's not nothing. *That is a gift* [emphasis added]."[12]

To learn more about the support of perinatal hospice, watch inspiring videos of people who chose that life-affirming path, and get in-depth answers to questions and information about programs around the world, go to www.perinatalhospice.org.

[12] Byron C. Calhoun, "The Perinatal Hospice: Allowing Parents to Be Parents," Charlotte Lozier Institute, May 1, 2012, https://lozierinstitute.org/the-perinatal-hospice/.

When Our Bodies Become Crime Scenes

The magnolia tree magnifies
My babies buried beneath

One Saturday morning in September 2022, a few friends and their children arrived at our home. They were dressed in their finest. Then our priest friend arrived. We proceeded to our home office which overlooks our sprawling, tropical backyard. My desk happens to face east, so it was transformed that morning into an altar. Upon it lay one of my husband Joe's cigar boxes, which he had sanded down the night before. It was wrapped in a family heirloom—the white, hand-knit blanket from my sister's and my baptisms. Inside rested the remains of Michael (pronounced the Hebrew way of *me-khah-eyl*), our baby who left my body too soon.

Father donned his vestments. The funeral Mass began.

This was the second child Joe and I had buried. And it wasn't only we who wept after Mass when we processed to bury Michael under the magnolia tree, alongside his oldest sister, LaeLae, whom we had laid to rest two years

79

prior. Tears flowed from our friends, too, because they knew the precious gift of children and understood the great sorrow that is miscarriage.

I regularly speak of my children whom I didn't get to hold. When I am in the grocery store with my two-year-old and people ask, "Is she your first?" I always say, "No, my first is in heaven. Then Violet came right after." We have a canvas on our wall that marks the short life of LaeLae. We bought a sleeper for Violet to wear that says "Little Sister" because we want to acknowledge there was a sibling before her.

When Violet's first birthday came along, we wrote a card that said, "You're a big sister," announcing to friends and family that we were pregnant again. When we lost Michael a short while later, we printed a canvas for him too.

Then there was Ollie. We rejoiced with such hope that we were blessed to get pregnant again, and we prayed this little one would stay the course. But once again, an ultrasound and bloodwork sadly showed otherwise, and shortly after, the bleeding began.

After that I became pregnant for a fifth time. We nicknamed that little one "Job" for the end of Job's story in the Bible when "the Lord restored the fortunes of Job" and "gave Job twice as much as he had before" (Job 42:10). We saw Job on ultrasound twice and heard his heartbeat. My belly swelled. I experienced morning sickness. But at a routine twelve-week pregnancy checkup, we were stunned to discover Job had died. It took three weeks of waiting before my body began labor to deliver Job, and another two weeks for the miscarriage to complete.

I read somewhere that one in five pregnancies ends in miscarriage. For me, four out of my first five did. So now, when people ask how many children I have, my answer is "Six. Four are in heaven."

I raise the topic of miscarriage because one of the fears some abortion supporters have spread after the Dobbs decision is that in states where abortion is restricted, women who miscarry may find themselves in jail, charged with ending their child's life. That is fearmongering misinformation. There is a profound difference between a child dying naturally and one who is killed purposefully (just like there is a difference between someone having a heart attack versus someone being stabbed in the heart).

As a pro-life woman who has miscarried four times, I have no guilt that I did something wrong, nor do I fear that I could face fines, trials, or prison. During all four of my miscarriages, I was under constant medical attention, getting ultrasounds and bloodwork, going to doctors' offices and the hospital. Not once did I ever sense that the physicians, nurses, phlebotomists, or ultrasound technicians were suspicious that my pregnancy losses were somehow self-inflicted crimes.

Analogously, consider parents whose toddler breaks her leg. When they rush her to the hospital, they don't fear the hospital investigating them for child abuse. Is it possible a child who presents with a broken leg was intentionally harmed by someone? Yes, that is *possible*, but generally parents do not do that to their children. If authorities suspect abuse, that's because there are other suspicious signs besides a broken bone. And even when such a possibility exists, in a civil society, one is always innocent until proven guilty.

We should not fear that authorities will consider our bodies crime scenes when a miscarriage occurs. The same cannot be said about abortion though. Abortion is intentional. It is an attack—on one's child as well as on one's nature as a mother, who is meant to give her body for her child, not destroy her child's body for herself. Abortion is so tragic because it is the opposite of the communing and bonding we were made for; instead, it separates and destroys. Even when abortion occurs in places where it is legal and thus not considered a "crime" by a technical definition, one could say abortion is always a moral crime because it is a grave offense against human persons and human dignity.

"So what should we do to women who have abortions? Should they go to jail?"

Those are questions abortion supporters often ask me. When responding, I think it's helpful to get behind the words in order to discover the motivation for the questions.

Why is this person asking me this question? If a pro-lifer responds that women who have abortions should *not* go to jail, abortion supporters may reply, "Ah! Then you can't really believe abortion is homicide because in other cases of homicide, you would put the guilty party in prison." If a pro-lifer says women who have abortions *should* go to jail, abortion supporters may reply, "What?

You're cruel and insane. That's a large percentage of women—our mothers, sisters, aunts, and others—and our jails would overflow."

In either case, it seems abortion supporters ask the question in order to "catch" the pro-lifer, to make her look inconsistent, bad, or both, and they hope a listening audience will reject the pro-life perspective as a result. It's weak argumentation because it does not follow that abortion is acceptable if pro-life people are inconsistent or if pro-life people appear, or even are, insensitive.

It is worth remembering that most women who have had abortions have done so in a climate where abortion is legal, so although a *moral* crime occurred, a *legal* crime did not, so there are no legal consequences to implement. Even where a legal crime does occur, whether a victim is pre-born or born, authorities need to determine whether an involved party is criminally responsible, whether there was coercion, consent, and to what degree, if any, there was culpability. So yes, civil societies should be consistent and have penal consequences for someone who intentionally kills a human, regardless of the victim's age, but that comes after a fair investigation and trial.

But such a trial isn't going to occur as long as abortion is allowed. So the first hurdle to jump is not a question of legal consequences for women but a question of legal protections for the pre-born.

In other words, if two people are debating what the legal consequences should be for women who have abortions but one person believes abortion is a woman's right, then that individual is *not* going to be convinced of giving *any* legal punishment to women. The main strategy in such an encounter, then, should be to convince the person that abortion is a grave wrong. Only *after* we agree upon this is it reasonable to discuss, debate, and theorize what the reasonable and just consequences would be under some future law.

Therefore, when having that first conversation about the immorality of abortion itself, I think there's a vital question that *we* should bring to the discussion. Instead of focusing on the question of what we should do to women who have abortions, we need to ask, "What should we *say* to women who have had abortions?"

The answer has already been said. By a saint. And it's worth repeating. In the encyclical letter *Evangelium Vitae,* St. John Paul II wrote,

> I would now like to say a special word to women who have had an abortion. The Church is aware of the many factors which may have influenced your decision, and she does not doubt that in many cases it was a painful and even shattering decision. The wound in your heart may not yet have healed. Certainly what happened was and remains terribly wrong. But do not give in to discouragement and do not lose hope. Try rather to understand what happened and face it honestly. If you have not already done so, give yourselves over with humility and trust to repentance. The Father of mercies is ready to give you his forgiveness and his peace in the Sacrament of Reconciliation.

To the same Father and his mercy you can with
sure hope entrust your child. With the friendly
and expert help and advice of other people, and
as a result of your own painful experience, you
can be among the most eloquent defenders of
everyone's right to life.[1]

That's right—the mother who turned her body into a
crime scene and ended her child's life can be transformed
into the most eloquent defender of life. I have witnessed
the truth of that statement in my partnering with various
post-abortive women in pro-life outreach over the years.
I once gave a pro-life apologetics talk at a high school
alongside a woman who shared her testimony of regret-
ting abortion. As a result, a teenager in the audience who
was pregnant decided to carry her baby to term.

On another occasion, I participated in a pro-life display
where a passerby who had had an abortion was filled with
conviction and sudden grief over what she had done. One
of our team members, decades prior, had had an abortion
herself, and she was the one to minister to that woman.

Or I think of a woman from Toronto, Canada, named
Debbie Fisher. She shared her testimony of abortion regret
at a high school where a student had a friend who was,
at that moment, on a bus to an abortion clinic. The student called the girl and said, "There's a woman here that

---

[1] Pope John Paul II, Encyclical on the Value and Inviolability of Human Life
Evangelium Vitae (March 25, 1995), §98, http://www.vatican.va/content/
john-paul-ii/en/encyclicals/documents/hf_jp-ii_enc_25031995_evangelium-
vitae.html.

regrets her abortion."[2] The pregnant teen was willing to meet with Debbie, and after sharing her fears and listening to Debbie's story, she chose life, delivering a baby girl several months later.

A response of mercy can be bewildering to abortion supporters. But to pro-life Christians it is not, because we embrace the *Good News*—that is, the message "For God so loved the world that he gave his only-begotten Son, that whoever believes in him should not perish but have eternal life" (John 3:16). What could be better news than finding out that, even with all our sins, we won't have to bear the consequence of death, because someone else has loved us enough to spare us by taking our consequence upon Himself? What could be better news than hearing that we have the chance to spend eternity in perpetual light rather than unending misery?

When religious teachers of His day approached Jesus because they were appalled that Jesus was welcoming sinners and eating with them, Jesus responded to the leaders' disdain by saying,

> What man of you, having a hundred sheep, if he has lost one of them, does not leave the ninety-nine in the wilderness, and go after the one which is lost, until he finds it? And when he has found it, he lays it on his shoulders, rejoicing. And when he

[2] Renata Iskander, "Five Minutes from Abortion, Students Save Woman from Tragic Mistake," *The Interim*, August 7, 2013, http://theinterim.com/issues/society-culture/five-minutes-from-abortion-students-save-woman-from-tragic-mistake/.

comes home, he calls together his friends and his neighbors, saying to them, "Rejoice with me, for I have found my sheep which was lost." Just so, I tell you, there will be more joy in heaven over one sinner who repents than over ninety-nine righteous persons who need no repentance. (Luke 15:4–7)

We are all sinners who need to repent. Whether the sin is abortion or something else, we all need God's mercy. The good news is He is willing to bestow it. And His mercy not only forgives; it also transforms.

In 1980, the Mount St. Helens volcano in Washington State erupted. My mom recalls that it was so loud that she, who was pregnant with me at the time, could hear it from almost four hundred miles away, across the border in Vancouver, Canada. This natural disaster caused great devastation, which can act as a metaphor for sin in our lives, including the sin of abortion. The Sisters of Life offer a powerful perspective on this. They write,

The eruption of Mt. Saint Helen's triggered the largest landslide in recorded history, toppling 4 billion board feet of timber and landscape for 230 square miles, and sending 520 million tons of ash into the air darkening skies 250 miles away. The area was entirely devastated. And yet, thirty-five years later life has returned.

And though the old scenery has passed, a new landscape and ecosystem has emerged, witnessing to the tenacious capacity of life to recover even after disaster . . .

When our lives are challenged to rise forth from the ashes—we can cling with confidence to the possibilities of the life-giving power of Christ's resurrection. When pain and affliction erupt into our lives and threaten our every sense of security and wellbeing—we can let Love go to work redeeming every place with His infinite and inexhaustible mercy. When death touches us through sin and illness—we can lay its every sting to rest in the tomb with Our Redeemer, and wait for it to burst forth into new life with Him. When the unexpected breaks our lives into pieces and clouds our every hope—we can choose to abide in Jesus Christ—the Savior who is with us, and whose Sacred Heart beats within us as much as our very own, trusting, He will make all things new.[3]

The sisters' words about the transformation of the area around Mount St. Helen's after the explosion are words of encouragement for all of us burdened by regrets in our past: "a new landscape and ecosystem" can emerge and give witness to "the tenacious capacity of life to recover even after disaster." There is hope. Our story does not need to end in disaster.

[3] Sister Mariae Agnus Dei, SV, "Claiming Redemption in Every Part of Our Lives," *Imprint*, Fall 2016, https://sistersoflife.org/wp-content/uploads/2019/05/FALL-2016-1.pdf.

And that brings to mind two questions my tenth grade religion teacher asked my class to focus on for the year:

1. What kind of person am I becoming?
2. What kind of person do I want to become?

These questions are key because they orient us to reflect on what we can control—the present and future—rather than what we cannot control—the past. The woman who has had an abortion cannot bring her baby back to life. But she can reflect on what kind of person she is becoming right now, and she can make a decision to be different in the present moment, to speak up for *other* pre-born children the way she wished she had for her own. This way, the type of person she becomes in the present and future is a *rescuer* (of other pre-born children at risk of losing their lives), a *protector* (of women at risk of being harmed by abortion), and a *nurturer* of life overall. In short, the body that was once a crime scene can be transformed into a body that is a safe haven.

On a practical level, how does such a transformation unfold? The first thing to realize is that healing takes *time*. The Sacrament of Reconciliation washes away our sins through the blood of Christ, but tendencies and habits can remain. After we repent, we should seek out people and programs that can help us work through why we made the choices we did, to consider what aspects of our past decisions, family of origin, and life experiences can give insight into our behavior, and then to develop a plan for cultivating virtue based on this knowledge and our unique temperament.

Consider the healing of physical wounds, which can require surgery, physiotherapy, stitches, antibiotics, bandages, ointments, and so forth, all of which take time to bring about the desired effect. So it is with our spiritual healing. We must take various steps to bring about restoration. Besides making use of the sacraments, these steps can include private therapy, group therapy, spiritual direction, Bible studies, retreats, prayer groups, and conferences. Pursuing these approaches inevitably involves accompaniment—the presence of others who guide, mentor, or sit alongside us as we journey to peace. Having others accompany us through this process reinforces God's declaration in Genesis 2 that man was not meant to be alone and that, particularly in our brokenness, we need communion with others.

A Post-Roe Application

With abortion access varying among states and the political landscape continually shifting, the news media increasingly features the topic of abortion. This can act as a trigger for those who have had or have facilitated abortions and who live with unresolved regret. Many suffer silently, haunted with reminders, but they don't know how to handle the pain they are experiencing.

To help such individuals find healing, churches and pro-life organizations need to be at the forefront of raising the issue and speaking to the silently suffering, providing opportunities for repentance and healing. I was reminded of this need when, several years ago, I gave a pro-life presentation at a church. These were some of the encounters I had with audience members afterward:

- A woman in her seventies came up to me at the table and said she had an abortion decades ago. I asked her if she would be open to post-abortion counselling, and she said, "Do you think it would be good?" I said yes, that closure was important even if it was decades later. Speaking with her reminded me of a woman in her eighties who once heard me speak about abortion at a women's conference. She pulled me aside and whispered something she had never told another soul—that decades earlier, she had had an abortion.

- A man said he was interested in reading my book to get ideas for how to help his daughter, who had an abortion eight years prior. As he shared, he said he was particularly struck when I spoke about being silent when we should have spoken up. He got choked up, convicted of his own silence at a pivotal moment in his daughter's life, and walked away weeping.

- I spoke with a married couple who have a blended family, and the husband's daughter, years ago, had had an abortion without his knowledge at the time. The girl's mom, the man's ex-wife, didn't want him to know because she knew he wouldn't support the abortion. Another daughter of theirs (of the newly married couple) got pregnant as a teenager, and this couple adopted their grandchild, who is now an adult and married with her own kids. As the mom said, "I won't help my daughter kill, but I will help my daughter live."

- One woman said to me, "I don't think anyone I know has had an abortion." I told her that statistically, she likely *did* know people but that they simply haven't told her. Another woman in our conversation, who is a maternity nurse, echoed my sentiment, saying that she sees women's medical records and how a surprising number of them show "TA" (therapeutic abortion). She remembers one patient history that indicated a TA, and then in big letters underneath, it said, "HUSBAND DOES NOT KNOW."

These encounters reinforced what I had observed for some time—that there are so many walking wounded in our midst. After that experience, I decided to develop a simple memorial service template for churches. When I piloted it at one parish, over one hundred people flocked to the church to honor and remember aborted children. The experience reinforced that everyone has a story. One person had, decades before, paid for a woman's abortion. Another person's mother had almost been aborted.

Another person tried to dissuade someone from support-ing a friend's abortion—and failed.

The stories go on, showing that while some have directly had abortions, all have been touched by abortion in some way. The memorial was a way of responding to these experiences. As one attendee said afterward, "I've experienced a healing and will sleep better tonight than I have in years." This event was extremely low cost, did not involve much work, and was very powerful.[4]

Pro-life supporters have developed various other events, programs, and organizations, and the time is ripe to make use of them. These include the Silent No More Awareness Campaign, Rachel's Vineyard, Project Rachel, and Hope and Healing with the Sisters of Life, as well as And Then There Were None, which is an outreach specifically designed to help abortion clinic workers who leave the industry.

---

[4] For those who are interested in planning and delivering a memorial service for aborted children, you can view the template on my website: https://loveunleasheslife.com/blog/2016/6/15/a-step-by-step-guide-to-planning-and-delivering-a-memorial-service-for-aborted-children.

5

The Greatest Example of "My Body for You"

"I thank you for your forgiveness that I may go to the Day of Atonement with a lighter conscience."[1]

In the spring of 2017, I went to the home of Orthodox Jewish friends of mine, whom I will call Jake and Sarah, to celebrate Passover. I marvel at how that encounter even happened, because almost twenty years prior, things were hostile between Jake and me.

To go back to the beginning, in 1999, I was a second-year undergraduate studying at the University of British Columbia (UBC) in Vancouver, Canada. I was the president of the pro-life club, and that fall, a group of us pro-life students decided to display images from the Genocide Awareness Project (GAP) on campus. We knew the pro-life message was controversial, but GAP took things to a whole new level. The display showed abortion-victim photography alongside images of other human rights violations.

[1] E-mail to Stephanie Gray, August/September 2007.

95

Our point was this: just as it is wrong to deprive humans of their personhood based on skin color, religion, or ethnicity (as was historically the case with Blacks during slavery, Jews during the Holocaust, and Tutsis during the Rwandan genocide), so, too, is it wrong to deprive humans of their personhood based on age, which is what is happening to the pre-born in abortion.

When people deny personhood status to the pre-born because they aren't conscious or cannot feel pain, for example, we need to remember that embryos and fetuses are less developed in those areas simply because they are younger. To deny them legal personhood status because they lack a more mature level of intellectual development, for example, is to exclude them based on how old they are, which is age discrimination.

Moreover, when human rights violations occur, we often hear dehumanizing rhetoric against the victims. For example, Jews were called rats, Tutsis were called cockroaches, and pre-born children have been called parasites, which supposedly justifies the widespread killing ("extermination") of the targeted group.

Comparing different injustices is not new. When I attended UBC, the Jewish club, Hillel, compared the Rwandan genocide to the Holocaust and hosted a speaker who said, "'Never again' doesn't just mean 'never my people.' It means never again for all people, for all of humanity." Several years later, I went to the Holocaust Memorial Museum in Washington, DC, and observed that amidst the memorials of the Jewish Holocaust was an exhibit showing images of more recent atrocities, including pictures from Rwanda's genocide. A quote in that section by Holocaust survivor Elie Wiesel said the following: "A memorial unresponsive to the future would violate the memory of the past." Then, several years after that, I took a trip to Poland and visited Auschwitz, which had on display a quote by George Santayana: "The one who does not remember history is bound to live through it again."

For these reasons, our club displayed the message we did, including abortion among other human rights atrocities; however, the message was received with great resistance. I suppose when a culture looks with horror at some aspect of human history, it doesn't like to think it could be guilty of committing and permitting in the present moment something similar to actions it despises from the past.

And so, not only did our club face criticism over our claims but also threats to our right to freedom of speech. In fact, various students and campus groups attempted to censor our freedom of expression. We were in almost every issue of the campus newspaper, and abortion debate on campus was constant. There were countless meetings with university administration, campus police, and campus security. Some students even violently attacked our first display, leading to national media coverage.

Fast forward to 2007, and I was several years post-graduation, working full-time in the pro-life movement. I was still connected to the UBC pro-life club, and they forwarded an e-mail to me from Jake, who had been at UBC when I was there. He requested that they pass his message along to me. He wrote,

During my tenure at UBC and on [boards of campus groups], I lobbied against Lifeline UBC's invitation of GAP because I felt, as a first generation Canadian, and child of a [Holocaust] survivor, that the concentration camp imagery juxtaposed with abortion imagery was insulting to the memory of my family members who both survived and perished during the genocide. I agreed with the idea behind it, as I have always been pro-life, save specific circumstance [sic], but felt that the method was wrong.

Since leaving UBC, getting married and having my own child, I have come to realize the error of my rationale, in fact, I now view my acts to prevent GAP . . . to be one of my big regrets from my time at UBC. I wish to apologize.[2]

I was stunned. I had no recollection of Jake specifically but had clear memories of all the hostility and censorship I'd faced as though it was yesterday. After I accepted his apology, Jake e-mailed me more about his change of heart. He told me that while attending a synagogue in a different part of Canada, he saw a flyer about a group in Israel that helps women carry through with their crisis pregnancies. He mentioned that the flyer indicated a high number of abortions of Jewish babies in Israel over the years, which struck him deeply. He wrote,

[2] E-mail to the UBC pro-life club, forwarded to Stephanie Gray, August 2007. He wrote to the club, "I wish to apologize to Lifeline UBC as well as apologize to Ms. Stephanie Gray who runs the display."

It was then that I realized that it was as a holocaust. There have been arguments about the Silent Holocaust being intermarriage, but no child dies with that, rather, children are born who are just not Jewish, but through abortion these are lives that just would not be. If this was just Israel, how many children could there have been with world Jewry? That was 2004.

Please let me know when your presentation will be in Vancouver next, I would like to see it and have the opportunity to apologize to you in person. As a final thought, The Torah teaches that in the time between Rosh Hashanah and Yom Kippur, one should ask their fellow person for forgiveness. Though this is early as Rosh Hashanah isn't until the 12th of September and Yom Kippur the Friday night of the following week, I thank you for your forgiveness that I may go to the Day of Atonement with a lighter conscience.[3]

As a result of Jake's e-mail, I met him and his family on several occasions over the years. This culminated in their invitation for me to join them for Passover in their home ten years after Jake sent his apology e-mail.

Given that we had been on opposite sides of the fence during our time at UBC, there was something especially powerful about uniting over a Passover supper. There I was, a Catholic Christian, and they, Orthodox Jews,

---

[3] E-mail to Stephanie Gray, around August/September 2007.

breaking bread, reading through the Old Testament story of our God's saving love for His people.

I've always loved the Exodus story of God rescuing the Israelites from slavery. In a world where people too often think miracles don't happen anymore, it's a great revealing of one epic miracle after another: leading the Israelites away from Egypt and toward the Promised Land by way of a column of cloud and a column of fire, the parting of the Red Sea, the provision of manna in the desert, providing water from a rock, and more. But before all of that, while the Jews were still in Egypt, God showed His mighty, saving hand.

When God prescribed to Moses and Aaron how the Passover ritual should occur, He told them to tell the Israelites that a family must

> take every man a lamb. . . . [It] shall be without
> blemish, a male a year old; you . . . shall kill their
> lambs in the evening. Then they shall take some
> of the blood, and put it on the two doorposts and
> the lintel of the houses in which they eat them.
> They shall eat the flesh that night, roasted; with
> unleavened bread and bitter herbs. . . . It is the
> Lord's Passover. For I will pass through the land of
> Egypt that night, and I will strike all the first-born
> in the land of Egypt, both man and beast; and on
> all the gods of Egypt I will execute judgments: I
> am the Lord. The blood shall be a sign for you,
> upon the houses where you are; and when I see
> the blood, I will pass over you, and no plague

shall fall upon you to destroy you, when I strike
the land of Egypt. (Exod 12:3, 5–8, 11–13)

The Jews were saved by the blood of the lamb. Fast
forward generations, and the prophet John the Baptist
declares about his cousin Jesus, "Behold, the Lamb of
God, who takes away the sin of the world!" (John 1:29).
As a lamb's blood was once shed in Egypt and its body
consumed so that death would pass over the people,
so Jesus would be the new Lamb. His blood was shed
and He invites us to consume His body so eternal death
would pass us over.

Humanity's choice to sin is what separated us from God
and left us the consequence of death. But not wanting us
to suffer eternally, God sent His Son, Jesus, to take our
consequence of death upon Himself instead, thus opening
to us the gates of heaven. Jesus—God Himself—is the
greatest example of "This is my body given for you."
He didn't just command us to love. He demonstrated it:
"Greater love has no man than this, that a man lay down
his life for his friends" (John 15:13).

Since Jesus was a Jew, He lived out *"my body for
you"* in a Jewish context. Jews commemorated Passover
annually, slaughtering a lamb each time, but Jesus gave
His life during the season of Passover to convey that He
was the new Lamb who would give His body for others.
The Jews didn't only kill the lambs though. They also ate
them. Like the sacrifice of the lamb, Jesus became food
for us in a Jewish context. One Jewish writer provides

a powerful commentary on the importance of food in Jewish culture:

> It's a time-honored stereotype: "Did you eat yet? Do you want more? You should eat more, *bubbeleh*, you look so skinny!" The Jewish mother, anxiously begging her children, her family, and anyone else in her home to please eat more, to please be nourished (and maybe tell her how good her cooking is). We, as a people, care about making sure everyone is well-fed. The nourishment of ourselves and of others can be construed as an innately Jewish and feminist act. . . .
>
> I know that Jewish values demand that we make sure other people eat. It's even in the Torah—there are injunctions to leave the corners of your field unharvested for those who do not have harvests of their own. There is the requirement, known as *shmita*, to allow your lands to lie unfarmed once every seven years, to ensure that this land will still be usable for future generations.[4]

As a mother myself, I marvel at how much time centers around food each day—preparing it, cleaning it up, making sure my toddler is well-fed. Food is a necessity for life. Without it, we die. It shouldn't be surprising, then, that Jesus, having lived as a human who experienced

[4] Sophie Hurwitz, "How Will Your Jewish Mother Feed You on a Starving Planet?" *Jewish Women, Amplified* (blog), Jewish Women's Archive, May 30, 2019, https://jwa.org/blog/how-will-your-jewish-mother-feed-you-starving-planet.

how central food is for survival, would present Himself as food. In doing so, He made it abundantly clear that we humans are wholly dependent on Him to live.

But rather than require a regular blood sacrifice as a remembrance of Him, Jesus chose to transform a food which was accessible to all men and still part of Passover—bread—and to make it His body. By transforming bread (and wine), Jesus becomes our daily bread, a constant reminder of our total dependence on Him.

During Jesus's public ministry, in John 6, a large, hungry crowd gathered to listen to Him near the time of Passover. He performed a miracle by multiplying five loaves and two fish and not only fed five thousand people but also had leftovers. The next day, when the amazed crowd went looking for Jesus again, He said to them, "Do not labor for the food which perishes, but for the food which endures to eternal life, which the Son of man will give to you; for on him has God the Father set his seal" (John 6:27). In this context of the season of Passover, of hunger, of being fed, and of miracles, Jesus set the stage for presenting Himself as the Lamb to be slain, whose body is to be eaten and who is bread from heaven.

Here is how it unfolded: The crowd referred to their ancestors who ate manna in the desert—who had received "bread from heaven." This was the familiar story of the Israelites fleeing from slavery and of God providing for them. Jesus said to the crowd, "[I]t was not Moses who gave you the bread from heaven; my Father gives you the true bread from heaven. For the bread of God is that which comes down from heaven, and gives life to the world" (John 6:32–33). Upon hearing these words, the people requested, "Lord, give us this bread always" (John 6:34). So Jesus offered Himself:

> I am the bread of life. Your fathers ate the manna in the wilderness, and they died. This is the bread which comes down from heaven, that a man may eat of it and not die. I am the living bread which came down from heaven; if any one eats of this bread, he will live for ever; and the bread which I shall give for the life of the world is my flesh. (John 6:48–51).

This saying bewildered the crowd. Was Jesus suggesting that people become cannibals? Indeed, the people questioned it; some even left Jesus over it. Instead of providing clarification that would ease His hearers' concerns, Jesus reiterated, reinforced, and drove home His point:

> Truly, truly, I say to you, unless you eat the flesh of the Son of man and drink his blood, you have no life in you; he who eats my flesh and drinks my blood has eternal life, and I will raise him up at the last day. For my flesh is food indeed, and my blood is drink indeed. He who eats my flesh and drinks my blood abides in me, and I in him. As the living Father sent me, and I live because of the Father, so he who eats me will live because of me. This is the bread which came down from heaven,

not such as the fathers ate and died; he who eats this bread will live for ever. (John 6:53–58)

As one commentary explains, "The Greek word used for 'eats' (*trogon*) is very blunt and has the sense of 'chewing' or 'gnawing.'"[5] By Jesus's word choice, we see that He was conveying a literal mastication.[6]

Jesus not only wants us to realize our utter dependence on Him for eternal life, and He not only wants to be our food so we can become one with Him in order to be like Him, but He wants all of that to overflow into our witness of love like His: "If any man would come after me, let him deny himself and take up his cross daily and follow me" (Luke 9:23); and "You call me Teacher and Lord; and you are right, for so I am. If I then, your Lord and Teacher, have washed your feet, you also ought to wash one another's feet" (John 13:13–14).

Pregnancy, and motherhood in general, are powerful ways to do this. In fact, Jesus's own mother would be a witness to Him of the love He ended up teaching and demonstrating. Before Jesus gave His body for us, His mother gave her body for Him. Before we ate Jesus's body, He ate hers. Before blood and water gushed forth from His body (John 19:34), it poured forth in labor from hers. Before He surrendered, "[n]ot my will, but

---

[5] "Christ in the Eucharist," *Catholic Answers*, accessed on September 14, 2023, https://www.catholic.com/tract/christ-in-the-eucharist.

[6] For an excellent explanation for the meaning of John 6, see Tim Staples, "What Catholics Believe about John 6," Catholic.com, November 1, 2010, https://www.catholic.com/magazine/print-edition/what-catholics-believe-about-john-6.

yours, be done" (Luke 22:42), she submitted, "[L]et it be to me according to your word" (Luke 1:38).

Jesus's first home was His mother, and she responded to God's invitation to be such a sanctuary by saying, "I am the handmaid of the Lord" (Luke 1:38). Unlike the perverse story of *The Handmaid's Tale*, where women were slaves against their will, Mary was a true handmaid who freely chose to serve. And with Mary's consent of "let it be to me according to your word" (Luke 1:38), God saved man through the womb of a woman.

Jesus models the greatest love. And pregnancy—motherhood—are meant to mirror that love *(see Figure 1)*.

To reject pregnancy, then, is to reject the greatest love. A short video called "Opposites," produced by Abort73.com, makes this point. The video begins by stating that the opposite of love is hate. It then asks what the opposite of the greatest love is, making the point that if the greatest love is a willingness to lay down your life for another, then the opposite of that is to lay down another's life for yourself. So, it concludes, the opposite of the greatest love is abortion.[7] As Catholic apologist and philosophy professor Peter Kreeft also put it, "Abortion is the Antichrist's demonic parody of the Eucharist. That is why it uses the same holy words, 'This is my body,' with the blasphemously opposite meaning."[8]

---

[7] "Opposites," Abort73, March 21, 2013, YouTube video, https://www.youtube.com/watch?v=rTPVoRL1t5E&t=1s.

[8] Peter Kreeft, *Jesus-Shock*, quoted in William Wolfe, "Biblical Worldview: Understanding Abortion as a 'Religious Sacrament' of the Left," Standing for Freedom Center, March 21, 2023, https://www.standingforfreedom.

Figure 1

Jesus is the greatest example of the greatest love.	Motherhood is meant to mirror that.
Jesus, as God, humbled Himself by coming down to our human level. "Have this mind among yourselves, which was in Christ Jesus, who, though he was in the form of God, did not count equality with God a thing to be grasped, but emptied himself, taking the form of a servant, being born in the likeness of men. And being found in human form, he humbled himself" (Phil 2:5–8).	A mother, as a mature adult, humbles herself by coming down to the level, in so many interactions, of her immature child. "This great urge to love, to serve, to bend down, is God's own essence" (Max Scheler).
Jesus loves us whether we love Him or not.	A mother unconditionally loves her children even when they aren't developed enough to love back or when they misbehave.
Jesus literally gave us His body to eat in order to nourish and transform us.	Through pregnancy, a mother literally gives her body to her pre-born child to eat in order to nourish him.
Jesus sacrificed His life so we could have eternal life.	A mother sacrifices her life as she knows it so her children can flourish.

com/2023/03/biblical-worldview-understanding-abortion-as-a-religious-sacrament-of-the-left/.

Such stark insight may be piercing to those ravaged with regret over abortion. While the previous chapter aimed to provide consolation, it is worth returning to the story of Jake and Sarah for a closer look at how God brings beauty from ashes (Isa 61:3).

In the months preceding that Passover supper in 2017, I received a message from Sarah, who told me she was pregnant with their sixth child and that an ultrasound report came back with troubling signs of possible health problems for the baby. They had no plans to end their child's life; however, in having to interact with so many people in the maternal-fetal-medicine world, who are very used to abortion being an option, Sarah asked, "Do you have any resources—books or articles—that you can recommend on choosing life in these circumstances?"[9]

I sent her information and was again moved by a response from Jake. He messaged me the following:

> In Judaism we believe that everything happens for a reason, perhaps the reason I voted with [group name] the way I did all those years ago against the GAP display was so that I could contact you to apologize and thus have you in my life for this very moment. The things you have sent Sarah have really been a big help to her. We pray to *G-d* that everything will be fine. Thank you so very much for being an indispensable resource.[10]

---

[9] Facebook Messenger message to Stephanie Gray, January 31, 2017.
[10] Facebook Messenger message to Stephanie Gray, February 5, 2017.

Everything happens for a reason. It reminds me of the Exsultet, which is proclaimed at the start of the Easter Vigil and includes these powerful lines:

> O love, O charity beyond all telling,
>   to ransom a slave you gave away your Son!
> O truly necessary sin of Adam,
>   destroyed completely by the Death of Christ!
> O happy fault
>   that earned so great, so glorious a Redeemer![11]

What does it mean to refer to a sin as "necessary" or a fault as "happy"? Consider this insight from Dominican Friar Father Jonah Pollock:

> The sin of Adam was necessary so that it could be destroyed by the death of Christ. Adam's fault is happy because it necessitated Christ's redemption. The sin of Adam is greeted with jubilation because it created the problem to which Christ's redeeming death and resurrection is the solution. It brought on the disease for which Easter is the cure. To be sure, the sin of Adam is not itself good. It is not, in itself, a cause for rejoicing. It is, rather, an occasion for good. It is the tragic plot twist that sets the stage for the story's glorious resolution. Our rejoicing is therefore not that Adam sinned,

[11] "The Exsultet: The Proclamation of Easter," excerpted from the English translation of the Roman Missal (2010), accessed on September 14, 2023, https://www.usccb.org/prayer-and-worship/liturgical-year-and-calendar/easter/easter-proclamation-exsultet.

but that, out of Adam's sin, God brought about a greater good. Indeed, in the redeeming death and resurrection of Christ, God brought to humanity a good far greater than the paradise Adam lost by his sin. Adam's fault is happy because it is the occasion for the saving life, death, and resurrection of Jesus Christ. It is the first and most consequential human sin that, as a sickness calls for a remedy, called forth the greatest and most consequential act of love.[12]

This is indeed good news. And particularly, it is good news for anyone ravaged with regret from abortion. As God brought good out of the sin of Adam, He can bring good out of the sin of abortion. Neither Adam's sin nor abortion are to be celebrated. But in light of these past choices that cannot be erased, we are to focus on God's majesty and His glorious response of drawing great good out of terrible evils. It is how He showed us the greatest love. And we pay our respects for that sacrifice in turn by giving the greatest love to others. Indeed, that's what His mother Mary did.

When Mary consented to receive Christ in her body, she was living out words her Son would declare decades later: "*This is my body given for you.*" In that moment of the Incarnation, she both received into her body and she gave of her body. She continued in that spirit of receiving

---

[12] Fr. Jonah Pollock, "O Happy Fault!" Dominican Friars Province of St. Joseph, March 30, 2016, https://opeast.org/2016/03/o-happy-fault/.

and giving when she learned of her cousin Elizabeth's pregnancy. In receiving the love and life of God, she then visited Elizabeth and gave the presence of Jesus to her. (That's why John the Baptist leapt for joy in Elizabeth's womb upon Mary's arrival—because he recognized the embryonic Christ child, whom Mary brought to them through her body.) There was Mary, in her first trimester, helping her cousin in her third trimester. Having received God's love for herself, she imparted God's love to others. Love always multiplies.

I like how St. Mother Teresa once put it when reflecting on this encounter of the cousins. When she gave a graduation address in 1982 at Thomas Aquinas College, she reflected on the newly pregnant Mary visiting Elizabeth and said, "Immediately she went in haste to give him to others."[13] As she spoke as a spiritual mother to students on the cusp of a new chapter in their adult lives, she told them to be like Mary and to be "carriers of God's love."[14] Isn't that what St. Mother Teresa herself was when she tirelessly served the poor, abandoned, and crippled? Isn't that what all people, and particularly pregnant mothers, are called to be? Carriers of God's love. When what we carry is special, even sacred, then to be given the opportunity to hold, to present, to *carry,* is a profound honor.

---

[13] Mother Teresa of Calcutta, "Commencement Address of Teresa of Calcutta at Thomas Aquinas College," September 1, 2016, YouTube video, https://www.youtube.com/watch?v=M5rQZVJv3h0.

[14] Teresa of Calcutta, "Commencement Address."

A Post-Roe Application

In the days leading up to the release of the Dobbs decision, the United States Conference of Catholic Bishops launched a National Eucharistic Revival for a three-year period beginning in June 2022. The initiative was designed to enkindle "a living relationship with the Lord Jesus Christ in the Holy Eucharist,"[15] and its timing amidst a fueled abortion debate seems divinely orchestrated.

Archbishop José Gomez of Los Angeles put it well when he said,

> The Eucharist is the gateway key to the civilization of love that we long to create. Jesus promised that he would be truly present in the sacrament of the altar—but also in the flesh and blood of our neighbors, especially those who are poor and suffering. If we ever hope to end human indifference and social injustice, then we need to revive this sacramental awareness. In every human person we meet—from the infant in the womb to our elderly parents drawing their dying breaths—we must see the image of the living God.[16]

During this season when Catholic parishes across the country are doing more education about the Real Presence

---

[15] "USCCB's National Eucharistic Revival Prepares for Highly Anticipated Launch During Feast of Corpus Christi," National Eucharistic Revival, June 6, 2022, https://www.eucharisticrevival.org/press-releases/usccbs-national-eucharistic-revival-prepares-for-highly-anticipated-launch-during-feast-of-corpus-christi.

[16] "USCCB's National Eucharistic Revival."

of Jesus in the Eucharist and are offering more adoration, Mass, and Reconciliation, this is a powerful time to commit to entering into more prayer, during Eucharistic adoration in particular. We should seize the opportunity to meditate more deeply on the greatest love of Christ and how our call to be mothers and fathers (spiritual or biological) is meant to mirror His message of *"This is my body given for you."*

To enter more deeply into a study and understanding of this greatest love of Christ, these books will be helpful: *The Fourth Cup: Unveiling the Mystery of the Last Supper and the Cross* by Scott Hahn; and *Jesus and the Jewish Roots of the Eucharist: Unlocking the Secrets of the Last Supper* by Brant Pitre.

6

When Our Bodies Are Invaded

If "my body for you" is a magnetic demonstration of something that is beautiful, then "your body for me" becomes something that is repulsive. And those who support abortion would rightly say the latter is perfectly synonymous with rape. "Shouldn't victims of sexual assault who get pregnant be allowed abortions?" they may ask. "After all, such women are innocent. Their bodies were invaded. They did not consent to the act which brought about pregnancy."

Responding to such a question is perhaps one of the greatest challenges pro-lifers face. This is not because the answer is unclear but because emotions run high. Every person of goodwill agrees that rape is a horrific evil and the opposite of the greatest love. When someone has been victimized, we want to help them feel better, not make them feel worse. And often it seems like maintaining a pregnancy in such a situation would make someone feel worse. If we object to abortion in that case, it appears insensitive to the profound suffering a woman has gone through. And so, to answer the question about the morality of abortion in cases of rape, it is helpful to ask a series of questions.

Will abortion unrape a rape victim? I once remarked to an audience member that whether a victim of rape gets pregnant or not, the assault itself is a trauma that an abortion will not take away. She said in response, "Yeah, ten years and counting."

Or consider my friend and fellow speaker Lianna Rebolledo.[1] She was kidnapped and raped at age twelve. After her attackers released her from the torture, she found out she was pregnant. When a doctor offered her an abortion, she asked whether it would help her forget the rape and ease her pain and suffering.[2] She explained her thought process when the doctor replied no: "I thought to myself, why should I have an abortion if it's not going to help me forget the rape?"[3]

In fact, Lianna was so traumatized by the sexual assault that she considered suicide. But she chose not to kill herself because she didn't want death for her pre-born child, which her own suicide would most certainly bring about. She carried through with the pregnancy and chose to parent her daughter, for whom she is so grateful. In effect, then, her child that was conceived in rape became

---

[1] You can visit Lianna's website here: http://www.lovinglife.org.

[2] Pete Baklinski, "Pregnant after Being Violently Raped at Just 12-Years-Old, She Rejected Abortion: Now She Has No Regrets," Lifesite, January 30, 2015, https://www.lifesitenews.com/news/woman-who-chose-life-after-brutal-rape-at-12-has-no-regrets-says-her-daught.

[3] Leah Brown, "Rape Victim Says, 'I Would Go Through That Again Just to Know My Daughter,'" Texas Alliance for Life, March 3, 2015, https://www.texasallianceforlife.org/rape-victim/.

her motivation to continue living, and she credits her daughter for saving her own life.

Certainly there is no denying that different people will have different reactions to trauma. Consider the Rwandan genocide, when mass rapes occurred. One report estimates that over two hundred thousand women were raped and approximately twenty thousand pregnancies resulted.[4] One survivor, Jacqueline, was gang-raped and became pregnant with her daughter Angel. Although she was initially so traumatized by the assault (as well as the murder of her husband and children) that she tried to poison herself and Angel, she eventually entered counselling and "started to love" her daughter. She now feels Angel came from God.[5] With the right support and help, Jacqueline was able to distinguish the innocence of the child from the guilt of the father.

This leads to another question we can ask when confronted with the morality of abortion following a rape: *Is it possible to be pregnant from a much-hated sexual assault and yet be grateful for the resulting child?*

Consider the stories of Amanda Berry, Gina DeJesus, and Michelle Knight. These women were kidnapped (at the ages of sixteen, fourteen, and twenty-one, respectively) and subjected to repeated rapes and other horrifying torture by Ariel Castro. They survived more than nine years of inhuman abuse in his home in Cleveland, Ohio.

---

[4] Danielle Paquette, "Turning Pain into Hope," *Washington Post*, June 11, 2017, http://www.washingtonpost.com/sf/world/2017/06/11/rwandas-children-of-rape-are-coming-of-age-against-the-odds/?utm_term=.7b90fb2eefc7.

[5] Paquette, "Turning Pain into Hope."

Amanda became pregnant by Castro three years into her captivity. What was her reaction?

In the spring of 2006, Amanda learned from the news that her mother had died from a massive heart attack. Soon after, she discovered she was pregnant and wrote in her autobiography, "I think my mom sent this baby. It's her way of giving me an angel. Someone to help pull me through, give me a reason to fight."[6]

Indeed, in the book *Hope: A Memoir of Survival in Cleveland* that she penned with fellow survivor Gina, the women wrote about Amanda's child conceived in rape: "We are inspired every day by Jocelyn Berry, who was born on a Christmas morning in the house on Seymour Avenue. She made a dark place brighter, and in many ways helped save us."[7] Amanda also wrote of her daughter Jocelyn,

> I used to worry that if I had the baby it would remind me of him [Castro] for the rest of my life. But I don't anymore. This is my baby. I'm so close now. I am still pretty small, maybe a hundred and fifteen pounds, less than when I arrived here, but my stomach looks huge to me. I already feel more like "we" than "I." Whenever I'm sadder or more depressed than usual, or when he does something

---

[6] Amanda Berry and Gina DeJesus, *Hope: A Memoir of Survival in Cleveland* (New York, NY: Penguin Books, 2016), 142.

[7] Berry and DeJesus, *Hope*, vi.

especially mean and my hope starts slipping away,
I rub my belly and talk to my baby.[8]

After giving birth in the torture chamber, she wrote,

I crawl into bed with my new baby. As he fastens
the chain around my ankle, I think about my
daughter being born into this prison, and who her
father is. But I try to focus on happier thoughts:
She seems healthy and she's beautiful. I am going
to protect her, and the rest we will figure out as
we go.[9]

The experience of fellow survivor Michelle Knight was
very different. She became pregnant five times by Castro,
and he beat her each time, killing all her pre-born children in the process.[10] In fact, Castro was charged with
four counts of aggravated murder for this.[11] The jury's
decision on these charges leads to important questions:
Is killing wrong based on *who does* the killing or based
on *who* is killed? If it was wrong for Castro to kill the
children conceived in rape, wouldn't it be wrong for
anyone to kill children conceived in rape? Is the human

[8] Berry and DeJesus, *Hope*, 148.

[9] Berry and DeJesus, *Hope*, 152.

[10] Adam Carlson, "Cleveland Kidnapping Survivor Michelle Knight Got
Tattoos for 'Every Abortion' She Had While in Captivity," *People*, September
6, 2015, http://people.com/human-interest/ariel-castro-kidnapping-
survivor-michelle-knights-tattoos-after-captivity/.

[11] "Cleveland Kidnapping Fast Facts," CNN, April 28, 2022, http://www.
cnn.com/2013/07/26/us/cleveland-kidnappings-fast-facts/index.html.

right to life grounded in *being* human or grounded in the *circumstances* under which a human was conceived?

In her autobiography *Finding Me: A Decade of Darkness, a Life Reclaimed*, Michelle writes that when he attacked her with a barbell because she was pregnant, she screamed, "Stop it! Please don't kill my baby!"[12] On another occasion, after he kicked her in the stomach to kill another child she had conceived by him, she wrote,

> I stood up and stared into the toilet. I reached down and scooped my baby out of the water. I stood there and sobbed. . . . Death would have felt better than seeing my own child destroyed. I looked down at the fetus in my hands. "I'm so sorry this happened to you," I wailed. "I am so sorry. You deserved better than this!"[13]

Or consider the story of Jaycee Dugard. She was kidnapped in California at eleven years old and held for eighteen years by Phillip and Nancy Garrido. Also subjected to rapes and other unspeakable torture, Jaycee gave birth to her first child at fourteen and a second at seventeen. She writes of her daughters conceived in rape, "I had my girls to give me strength,"[14] and "I am thankful for my daughters."[15] Of her first pregnancy, she said,

[12] Michelle Knight, *Finding Me: A Decade of Darkness, a Life Reclaimed* (New York, NY: Weinstein Books, 2014), 135.

[13] Knight, *Finding Me*, 210–11.

[14] Jaycee Dugard, *A Stolen Life: A Memoir* (New York, NY: Simon & Schuster Paperbacks, 2011), xi.

[15] Dugard, *A Stolen Life*, 45.

"The connection I feel for this baby inside of me every time I feel it move is an incredible feeling."[16]

Jaycee also wrote, "How do you get through things you don't want to do? You just do. I did it because that was the only thing I could do. I would do it all again. The most precious thing in the world came out of it . . . my daughters."[17]

Some might point out that because these women were still held captive while enduring rapes and pregnancies, new life was a comfort and light in an environment of ongoing darkness and suffering, but that for rape victims who are no longer enduring victimization, a child is an unnecessary reminder. So the next question to consider is this: *What is more difficult to come to terms with—being an innocent who is hurt or hurting an innocent?*

My friend Nicole Cooley got pregnant from rape, and she had an abortion. Nicole said, "For me, having an abortion was like being raped again, only worse—because this time I had consented to the assault."[18]

Or consider Penny Ann Beernsten. She was raped in 1985. Unfortunately, she incorrectly identified an innocent man, Steven Avery, as her attacker.[19] He was imprisoned for eighteen years until DNA-testing technology identified the actual rapist, Gregory Allen. Penny wrote,

---

[16] Dugard, *A Stolen Life*, 99.

[17] Dugard, *A Stolen Life*, 110.

[18] Amy Reid, "Nicole Cooley: Raped and Pregnant," CBN, December 10, 2022, http://www1.cbn.com/700club/nicole-cooley-raped-and-pregnant.

[19] "Steve Avery," Innocence Project, accessed on September 14, 2023, https://www.innocenceproject.org/cases/steven-avery/.

> The day I learned of the exoneration was worse
> than the day I was assaulted. I really fought back
> when my attacker grabbed me. I scratched him,
> I kicked him. I did not go gently. After the DNA
> results came back, I just felt powerless. I can't
> un-ring this bell. I can't give Steve back the years
> that he's lost.[20]

While both these women went through horrifying traumas no human should ever have to endure, they acknowledged a worse pain when they realized that their own actions hurt other people. Of course, there is no denying the impact their traumas had on their judgment and the failure of those around them, who were emotionally removed from the situations, to better guide them, but the point still stands that it is more difficult to come to terms with hurting an innocent than in being an innocent who is hurt.

Another question to propose when considering the morality of abortion after rape is this: *Since the child conceived from rape will ultimately need to come out of the rape victim's body one way or another, which is better—to remove the child dead or alive?*

In a survey of 192 women who got pregnant from sexual assault, almost "80 percent of the women who aborted the pregnancy reported that abortion had been

---

[20] Christie Thompson, "Penny Beernsten, the Rape Victim in 'Making a Murderer,' Speaks Out," Marshall Project, January 5, 2016, https://www.themarshallproject.org/2016/01/05/penny-beernsten-the-rape-victim-in-making-a-murderer-speaks-out.

the wrong solution."[21] Of the women who gave birth to their children, none of them "expressed regret or wished they had aborted instead."[22]

The documentary *Allowed to Live: A Look at the Hard Cases* shares powerful stories of people who regret abortions after rape, rape victims who are grateful they carried their children to term, and children conceived by rape who are thankful their moms protected their lives.[23] This brings to mind my friend Ryan Bomberger.[24] He came into existence through rape, and his birth mother chose adoption. He was adopted into a loving family of thirteen children, with nine of those siblings being fellow adoptees.

Ryan's biological mother may have been a victim of "This is your body taken for me," but her choice to go through the hardship of pregnancy after rape is a powerful demonstration of "This is my body given for you." Although he has never reunited with his biological mother, Ryan continues her legacy of self-sacrificing love through adopting children of his own as well as speaking on behalf of vulnerable pre-born children.

The question of how to respond to pregnancies from rape is challenging because it is not just a matter of theory. It involves real people who have endured profound suffering and abuse. With love as our call, willing

[21] David C. Reardon, "Sexual Assault and Abortion Brief," Tennessee Right to Life, accessed on September 14, 2023, https://www.tnrtl.org/saab.

[22] Reardon, "Sexual Assault and Abortion Brief."

[23] "Allowed to Live: A Look at the Hard Cases," Conceived in Rape, August 17, 2015, YouTube video, https://www.youtube.com/watch?v=FfKkWfDEQjc.

[24] "About Ryan Bomberger," Radiance Foundation, accessed on September 14, 2023, https://radiancefoundation.org/ryan/.

that individual's good must be our goal in these encounters. The loving and good thing to do is not always easy. As the various stories in this chapter reveal, however, it is possible to choose the morally right path even in the face of much difficulty.

Pre-born children, like their mothers, are not the guilty parties in sexual assault, and we ought not to hold them responsible for a heinous crime they did not commit. Protecting pre-born life from harm the way one wishes she herself had been protected from harm brings an end to the perspective of "This is your body taken for me," and instead establishes a new story—the loving witness of "This is my body given for you."

A Post-Roe Application

Since the Dobbs decision was passed, various states have implemented measures to protect pre-born children from abortion. In some states, however, the new laws are not ideal, as, for example, they allow for abortions in certain circumstances, such as rape. What should the pro-life response to these imperfect laws be?

It is important to distinguish a political strategy from a moral position. Some might argue that, politically, it would be difficult at certain times and in certain climates to pass an outright ban on all abortions. In an effort to ban *some* abortions in order to make progress in saving some lives, however, we end up embracing the compromise law. When determining whether such a partial ban is ethical, we need to ask, "Is this new law introducing evil, broadening evil, restricting evil, or eliminating evil?"

If it is introducing or broadening evil, it would never be ethical to support. If, however, a law restricts an evil, and a politician has a goal to ultimately eliminate an evil, then we can support it. St. John Paul II provides guidance for this in his encyclical letter *Evangelium Vitae*. He writes,

> A particular problem of conscience can arise in cases where a legislative vote would be decisive for the passage of a more restrictive law, aimed at limiting the number of authorized abortions, in place of a more permissive law already passed or ready to be voted on. Such cases are not infrequent. It is a fact that while in some parts of the world there continue to be campaigns to introduce laws favouring abortion, often supported by powerful international organizations, in other nations— particularly those which have already experienced the bitter fruits of such permissive legislation— there are growing signs of a rethinking in this matter. In a case like the one just mentioned, when it is not possible to overturn or completely abrogate a pro-abortion law, an elected official, whose absolute personal opposition to procured abortion was well known, could licitly support proposals aimed at limiting the harm done by such a law and at lessening its negative consequences at the level of general opinion and public morality. This does not in fact represent an illicit cooperation

with an unjust law, but rather a legitimate and proper attempt to limit its evil aspects.[25]

What is key with St. John Paul II's statement is that he points out that a politician's moral position of objecting to all abortions should be clear. Supporting an imperfect law should be a step in the right direction but not the final destination. As long as laws allow for some abortions, there is political work to be done. A measure that has a degree of force is not a sign to pack up and go home; rather, it should be motivation to stay and finish the job.

To further understand this point, we can use an analogy to another time in history, such as when slavery was allowed. If a state that allowed for enslavement of *all* Black people was going to implement a law that would protect *some* Black people, that would be a step in the right direction because it would be restricting the evil. Having said that, a politician of goodwill should continue to work to ensure legal protections for *all* Black people. The same is true for the pre-born.

---

[25] Pope John Paul II, Encyclical on the Value and Inviolability of Human Life Evangelium Vitae (March 25, 1995), §98, http://www.vatican.va/content/john-paul-ii/en/encyclicals/documents/hf_jp-ii_enc_25031995_evangelium-vitae.html.

7

When Our Bodies Are Broken

*"Today, my pregnant wife had her first ultrasound. . . .
We were shocked to find that my wife is pregnant with
triplets! But the joy . . . was cut short. The doctor told
us that we had a very rare situation. We have one baby
who is a singleton, and the other two are identical. The
problem is that they separated later in the pregnancy,
and there is no membrane separating the two. One
identical baby is much smaller (baby A), and the
other is much larger (baby B). And then baby C is just
hanging out in the corner with no health issues. The
doctor told us that we have decisions to make. Bringing
all three to term is very risky. It could mean that none
of them survive. It could also mean that those that do
survive have severe medical issues caused by the lack of
access to blood (the two identicals have their umbilical
cords twisted together). They have not recommended
anything, but there is a very clear implication that, if
we want to have a single healthy baby, then we need to
'reduce' the other two."*[1]

---

[1] E-mail to Stephanie Gray Connors, May 17, 2022.

A month before the Dobbs decision was released, the above e-mail was awaiting my attention. A teacher whom I had never met had followed my lectures online, even using a portion of one of my debates to teach his students about the art of arguing. But moral dilemmas were no longer just theoretical for him; he and his wife were living one out.

What is the right thing to do when our bodies are broken? In other words, in the presence of illness, disease, or something that has gone wrong in the body, and pre-born children could die, be disabled, or have shorter-than-normal lives, what is the moral course of action? Or what if there is a risk a pregnant woman could die? What is the ethical thing to do then?

Situations like these are difficult precisely because all involved are valuable human beings. When people are loved, we don't want them to die. And so we want to try to save peoples' lives. The challenge always is this: *How* may we save someone's life? Are there some approaches that are off limits to us, as good as our intentions may be?

As we explore this, let's begin by returning to the parents, Robert and Joannah, and their triplets. We can learn a lot about the right principles to embrace when considering a particular case study like theirs. I told Robert that not being able to save one was very different from directly killing one—the latter always being wrong. But their situation was tough. Two of their babies had twin-twin transfusion syndrome (TTTS). The identical twins shared one placenta, but blood was not circulating evenly between them. One twin was getting too much blood, and the other was receiving too little. Their lives were in jeopardy.

Back and forth our exchanges went as I tried to help them process what they were facing and what the medical professionals were telling them. Robert and Joannah are Christian and pro-life and did not want to abort, but they were overwhelmed by the weight of the situation and faced doctors who had alluded to "reduction" and, in fact, had presented it as an option. I told them "reduction" was a euphemism for abortion and that they should not be misled by medical professionals who suggest it.

At one point Robert realized he didn't even know how reductions were done, so he searched online. He wrote,

> Once I Googled it, I began sobbing. I showed my wife, and we both just held each other for a while, crying. They inject the baby's heart with potassium chloride, along with a few other chemicals. I became quite resolute, in that moment, that I couldn't be part of that.[2]

Robert also wrote,

> I told [my wife] that I just can't support the decision to abort. It would haunt me for the rest of my life, and I think it would be a cause for resentment in our marriage. We have a very healthy

---

[2] E-mail to Stephanie Gray Connors, May 19, 2022.

relationship, but I think that would be a bell we could never unring.[3]

Joannah agreed. Moreover, when they spoke to one physician, he pointed out that if the identical twins were "reduced" in order to save the fraternal triplet, it was possible that would trigger a miscarriage and, Robert reported to me, "the healthy baby would be flushed out with the dead ones. Once he put it that way," Robert said, "I think it was a done deal. We had already made up our minds about the issue [no reduction], but this cemented it."[4]

There was a lot Robert said that is worth repeating, but this sentiment in particular deserves emphasis: "In some ways, it was very freeing [to take reduction off the table], because it means that now we can start looking for solutions that fit our framework."[5]

And that is key in these difficult pregnancies. Our disposition must always be oriented to valuing every life involved. We must commit to never intentionally destroying any individuals, no matter what good we think could come from such destruction. Once homicide (with whatever language it is dressed up in) is not an option, we are forced to get creative and try as hard as possible to find a solution that protects everyone. Such a solution might not be achievable in this imperfect world, but it is worth emphasizing that there is a distinct difference

[3] E-mail, May 19, 2022.
[4] E-mail, May 19, 2022.
[5] E-mail, May 19, 2022.

between being unable to save everyone versus directly targeting one (or more) for death.

As Robert and I communicated back and forth, he shared this important insight:

> It just didn't seem like we were doing our job as parents by not going out swinging. I don't want to be haunted by this for the rest of my life, and so I think the only way that won't happen is if I try everything within my power to keep as many people alive as possible. And I think I have to be ready to accept that might mean none of them survive. *But I owe it to them to try* [emphasis added].[6]

Amen. That is a father who is protecting his family. In affirming his attitude, I told him,

> Our goal in this life is not length of life; it is Heaven. For some, our earthly experience will be long; for others, it will be short. But for all, the goal is to know, love, and serve God and fulfill His unique mission for each of us. We don't know the specific mission of your little ones; we just know we must not interfere with it. Their ultimate mission is love and how that will be lived out is to be determined. But never should their mission be thwarted by a fellow human ending their lives.

---

[6] E-mail, May 19, 2022.

> When I think of our daughter LaeLae who we miscarried at six weeks, I've accepted she was not meant to live long but she did live mighty. I was pregnant with her during two significant debates that touched my opponents and audiences [when I made reference to that pregnancy within the debates].[7]

Robert and Joannah were wrestling with a lot. So much information was coming at them, and quickly too. One of the things they needed to think through was a possible scenario involving the smallest and weakest triplet. If it became obvious that the baby wouldn't make it and she would be strangled by the umbilical cord, would it be better to end her suffering faster than to let the baby die slowly?

Given Robert's background in teaching debate, he thought of an analogy:

> [That's] like looking out to the horizon on an ocean and seeing a swimmer frantically trying to not drown. They're so far away that you know they aren't going to make it, but you have a rifle in your hand, so you shoot them to put them out of their misery. . .While compassion was the intention, there are too many unknowns that *could* have happened. The person could suddenly learn how to float or maybe you misconstrued their

---

[7] E-mail from Stephanie Gray Connors, May 19, 2022.

struggles in the water. But even if none of that were the case, it still wouldn't be morally just.[8]

Robert's thought process was good. We don't always see the full picture, and we ultimately do not have a right to do what is wrong. At the same time, it is completely understandable to want to minimize someone's suffering. No parent wants their child to suffer. I often say, "We should aim to alleviate suffering but never to eliminate sufferers." I wrote to Robert and Joannah,

> I was reminded this morning of a touching short video of a couple who was told their baby would die at birth. It's a different situation from yours, but it's relevant because they didn't shorten their son's already short life; instead, they were able to say "the only thing Thomas [their son] will ever know is love."[9] I want to help you and your wife make sure, however long or short your sweet daughters live (and hopefully it is long), that all they will ever know is love.
>
> . . . I got an image this morning of Jesus on the cross and Mary at the foot of the cross. She had true compassion, which means "to suffer with." Just imagine the agony she felt watching her Son suffer and wanting so badly to take His

---

[8] E-mail, May 19, 2022.

[9] "Choosing Thomas: Inside a Family's Decision to Let Their Son Live, If Only for a Brief Time," *Dallas Morning News*, August 28, 2009, YouTube video, https://www.youtube.com/watch?v=ToNWquoXqJI.

pain away. But she did not interfere with His mission of love. Instead, she stood by His side and gave Him comfort by her presence.[10]

The point of sharing these exchanges is to demonstrate the type of thinking we should have when faced with a pregnancy where various lives are threatened. Moreover, it is very natural to be confused or have questions for which we don't fully have the answers while still committing to doing the right thing. In these ethically complex situations, the danger is not in asking questions; the danger is in embracing an answer that is morally wrong.

Because Robert and Joannah were not going to walk down the life-ending path of reduction, they began to walk down the life-giving path of ethical interventions. They learned of a perinatologist in their city who was renowned for his ability to do corrective surgery on babies in the womb. In a fascinating twist of connections, my sister-in-law's father was the physician who—sixteen years prior—had recruited the very surgeon Robert and Joannah were going to meet with. My sister-in-law's father described this surgeon as "one of the most skilled perinatologists in the world." And guess what his first surgery was when he was hired at that clinic so many years ago? It was for TTTS.

In a modern-day Esther story, it seemed as though this doctor had been raised up "for such a time as this" (Esth 4:14). And yet, the recommending physician told Robert

<hr>

[10] E-mail from Stephanie Gray Connors, May 19, 2022.

and Joannah that while this perinatologist was the *one* surgeon he thought might chance surgery, he warned them that he might not think it was doable in their case. At eighteen weeks into the pregnancy, Robert and Joannah had their specialist appointment. That surgeon agreed to try surgery—the next day!

The triplets were not out of the woods, but their TTTS was cured. The next hours, days, weeks, and months were touch-and-go, but remarkably, all three made it to birth and were delivered two and a half months *after* that incredible in utero surgery. Even more remarkably, although they were born at only one pound two ounces, two pounds fourteen ounces, and two pounds eleven ounces, all three were successfully cared for in a NICU and have made it home and are doing well.

So what are the takeaways from this?

1. Always maintain a disposition of refusing to kill and of trying to save everyone.

2. Recognize that all lives involved are made in God's image and are equal in value. Treat them that way.

3. Remember, it's possible to have a good outcome for everyone. At one point in Robert and Joannah's process, their smallest and weakest baby was given a fifty-fifty chance of survival as, after the surgery, she had only 15 percent of the placenta. Hers were not great odds, yet she survived.

4. This story is a beautiful blend of the hand of God and of skilled humans using their minds and modern technology to save lives. If, however, not all lives had been saved, there still would have been a profound difference compared to if the parents had chosen the path of homicide instead. Although loss of life would have happened each way (trying and failing *versus* homicide), in one case it would have been death despite efforts to save, versus death from direct killing. The grief between those scenarios would be profoundly different because only one of them would carry guilt.

5. These situations are not easy—in the moment and after. Robert and Joannah's story is an important reminder that doing the right thing is often very, very hard. As Robert said,

> We, as a family, did struggle. I wouldn't want someone to think that the decision to keep all three girls was as easy as a coin flip. We struggled to get daily household chores done because Joannah was exhausted and couldn't exert herself. We struggled when our oldest daughter couldn't play with her mom how she used to; Joannah was just too fragile. We went into survival

mode, and it was tough. I think, for us, that was a big part of the pregnancy. And I know that some people are more apt to reduce when they have multiples because they don't want to take care of that many children. We discussed the possibility of adoption, especially if they had severe development issues, knowing that we just wouldn't be able to handle it. But at the end of the day, we knew that we just couldn't do that. The struggle was, and still very much is, real.[11]

This couple is to be lauded for doing the right thing even when it was hard while being brutally honest about the challenges and complexities they faced. As people of goodwill using their example to inspire others, we ought to be careful not to sugarcoat these situations. We want to inspire people to do the right thing with the full knowledge that there will be obstacles and hardships along the way. That they considered adoption reinforces their hardship while also demonstrating that there are life-affirming alternatives to being unable to care for one's child. Whereas abortion communicates, *If I won't have you, I won't let anyone have you,* adoption communicates, *If I'm struggling to meet your needs, I will find someone who can fulfill them.*

[11] E-mail to Stephanie Gray Connors, April 24, 2023.

Robert further wrote me about their smallest triplet, who has faced the most health challenges:

> It's been a struggle for us, and we know that there might be some development issues. We knew that going into the decision to have all three babies. Only time will tell if that's the case, but, much like you mentioned about how life is not a movie with a happy ending, sometimes these moments are just more "real" than anything else. We love her, and even if she ends up with some severe neurological disorder, that doesn't mean that we made the wrong decision.[12]

I have stayed in touch with Robert and Joannah, and they have sent me beautiful photos and updates of their precious girls. They have shared the continued highs *and lows*, which reminds me that theirs is not only the story of our world but also the story of parenthood in particular—there are moments of profound joy and wonder inevitably punctuated by illness and other challenges that come with living in this broken world. We all will suffer, and my own triumphs and trials in motherhood have taught me that the key is learning to suffer well.

Parents may feel pressured to abort for other complex issues during pregnancy. One such case is if a child will die at birth or shortly thereafter. Some people believe there is no point in continuing such a pregnancy because "the

---

[12] E-mail, April 24, 2023.

baby will die anyway." But consider that every single one of us is going to die anyway. It is literally the fate of all. As pro-life apologist Scott Klusendorf has pointed out, why should those of us who live longer have a right to end the lives of those of us who live shorter? Yes, a child in the womb whose fate is death-at-birth will live a much shorter life than we who read this. But until that child dies naturally, what right do we have to end her life purposefully? Moreover, there is also the possibility that the child won't die at birth, as prenatal tests have been known to be wrong. But even *if* a test is accurate, having a shorter life does not grant others a license to commit homicide.

People may nonetheless be inclined to support abortion in these cases because they focus on the grief that will follow when the child is born dead. A couple of my relatives have had stillbirths, and from what I know of their experiences, there are no words to capture that type of grief. It is a sorrow carried in the heart throughout one's life.

Abortion, however, does not spare them of such grief; it simply brings it sooner. Instead of grieving at birth, you grieve at the abortion. You still remember the child's absence from family gatherings. You still long for someone who is not there. Moreover, a woman who has a stillbirth experiences grief but not guilt. A woman who has an abortion of a child with a poor prenatal prognosis will experience grief *and* guilt.

Another complex pregnancy that can arise is one in which a pregnant woman could die. Some might ask,

"Doesn't a woman have a right and duty to preserve the well being of her own body, and therefore, isn't such a woman justified in pursuing abortion?"

First, it is important to realize that in that situation, something has gone wrong in the context of a symbiotic relationship that is fundamentally right. In other words, fertility and pregnancy are a sign of the body working properly. The female body was designed to be pregnant, so we should be oriented to preserve the well being of both people who are designed to have such cooperative connectedness.

Human beings in general are not immune from sickness and disease. That means that just as a non-pregnant woman can get sick, so can a pregnant woman. She might face challenges because of something that has arisen in her body independent of pregnancy (such as cancer). Or she might face challenges because of something that has gone wrong with the pregnancy (such as the child implanting in the fallopian tube instead of the uterus). Or she might face challenges because a health condition in her body makes it difficult to handle a pregnancy (such as pulmonary hypertension).

Second, when faced with these types of scenarios, we need to begin with what our disposition should be. We need to view the pregnant woman and her child as equals. We need to value both lives. We should not directly kill either life, each of which is designed for this unique relationship of being connected together. Notice how this is in direct contrast to abortion where the pre-born child is considered inferior and his body is directly attacked.

Third, where a woman's life is in danger after a pre-born child is viable (meaning we have technology to keep the baby alive outside the womb) or we can wait to intervene on the woman's condition until after viability, the obvious and ethical intervention is to deliver the child and place the baby in an incubator, thereby providing needed medical help to both the child and the mother.

But what if the mother's life is in danger *before* viability? In such a situation, the challenge is that the baby needs the mother's body in order to survive, so if the mother dies, the baby dies too. What then?

Let's begin with the main principle that should guide our thinking: We may never do evil to bring about a good. If there are ethical interventions that can benefit one without directly and intentionally killing the other, then that is a reasonable course of action. But if the *only* way of benefitting one is to do evil to another, then that wouldn't be ethical. It can be helpful to consider this principle in light of an analogous thought experiment.

Imagine a woman has been arrested and taken to a concentration camp. She is standing in line holding her child when a guard says to her, "I am going to kill both you and your child; however, if you kill your child in front of me, I will let you live." Clearly it would be wrong for the mother to kill her child even though doing so would stop the guard from killing her. No matter how important it is to preserve one's life, we may not achieve that end by doing evil—namely, killing an innocent human being. Even if the woman had other children to care for, that still would not justify her preserving her own life *through* killing the innocent child in her arms. If she kills the child, she bears responsibility for the child's death. If the guard kills the child, *he* bears responsibility for the child's death. This shows us the difference between suffering evil (being victimized) and doing evil (being a victimizer).

Now certainly the woman could try various things to defend herself and the child against the aggression of the guard; the point is simply that the one approach that is "off limits" is defending her own life by directly killing the innocent child. Simply put, that would just not be ethical. Such situations, whether imagined or real, are tragic and heartbreaking, but as ethicist Fr. Tadeusz Pacholczyk remarked, "Better two deaths than the direct taking of innocent life."[13]

The same is true if the situation is a pregnant woman whose life is in danger. If the only way to save her own life is to directly and intentionally kill the pre-born child, she must reject that path and instead accept early death. That might be shocking for some, but we must remember what we read earlier in this chapter: our goal in this life is not length of life; our goal is heaven. Because of this, we do not preserve life at all costs if that cost is committing an immoral act. As Fr. Pacholczyk continued,

---

[13] Father Tadeusz Pacholczyk, "Difficult Pregnancies, Precarious Choices, and the Absolute Value of Innocent Lives," Catholic Education Resource Center, accessed on September 14, 2023, https://www.catholiceducation. org/en/science/ethical-issues/difficult-pregnancies-precarious-choices-and-the-absolute-value-of-innocent-live.html.

Directly killing an innocent human being, even in the hopes of saving his or her mother, is an instance of engaging in an intrinsic—or absolute—evil, even if good may follow. By always repudiating the direct killing of the innocent, and acknowledging that this represents an exceptionless norm, we set in place the framework to safeguard human dignity at its root. Affirming this most basic norm leads us away from the injustice of playing God with other people's lives. Such challenging "life of the mother" cases remind us of our own limitations, and the mystery of God's greater Providence, as we face the hard truth that, despite our best efforts, we may not be able to successfully "correct" every medical situation that comes our way.[14]

To understand this point, consider my cross-examination of late-term abortionist Dr. Fraser Fellows during an abortion debate we did in front of medical students back in 2011:

Me: Would you say that organ transplantation is a medical procedure?

Dr. Fellows: Is organ transplantation a medical procedure? Yes.

Me: And would you say that, for it to be done safely and effectively, it requires medical expertise and medical instrumentation?

---

[14] Pacholczyk, "Difficult Pregnancies."

Dr. Fellows: It does.

Me: In July 2006, the CBC reported allegations that the Chinese government was harvesting and selling the organs of practitioners of the spirituality Falun Gong. And the story indicates that allegedly these prisoners are being tortured to give consent for organ donation. The organs are taken from them; they are killed, and then obviously physicians would not only be involved in the removal of the organs but in the transplant into the other person. Would you say it is unethical for a physician to be involved in this medical procedure?

Dr. Fellows: I would.

Me: Okay. And so it's therefore possible for a medical person to do a medical act with medical instruments and it be unethical in some situations?

Dr. Fellows: Absolutely.[15]

As we can see from this exchange, even a man who makes a living ending the lives of pre-born children admits that not all medical acts are ethical. It simply would not be moral to give someone an organ transplant if the organ was obtained by way of harming or killing someone else. Likewise, it would not be moral to save a woman's life if we did so by way of homicide.

This, of course, is all principles and theory. What is it like in practice? As with the triplets, let's consider a case study—two, in fact.

---

[15] "Stephanie Gray vs. Dr. [Fraser] Fellows: Stephanie Gray Cross Examines Dr. Fellows," University of Western Ontario Medical School, January 2011, YouTube video, https://www.youtube.com/watch?v=tNAKPvV2YXY.

The first is about an Australian woman named Pamela Cook. In 2011, she entered the televised singing contest *The X-Factor* (Australian series) and shared what motivated her to pursue her dream of singing. She revealed that when she was in her late twenties, when she was sixteen weeks pregnant, she was diagnosed with breast cancer and was encouraged to "terminate the pregnancy."[16] She said that was not an option for her and the child's father. She continued the pregnancy as well as pursuing chemotherapy. Her baby boy, Zion, was delivered nine weeks early but is doing fine.[17] Through this she learned that life is short, and it inspired her to pursue her dream of singing. But her presence in the contest also provided a platform for her story of courage and love to be an inspiring witness to others.

Whenever people make decisions, they are guided by something. Even if we don't explicitly reference those guideposts, we all have worldviews and standards that influence how we think and behave. The Catholic Church is no different. It has a long history of appealing to natural law and has done an excellent job of clearly articulating its positions. It can be helpful to look at these in light of Pamela's story.

Take, for example, the document *Ethical and Religious Directives for Catholic Health Care Services*, produced by the US Conference of Catholic Bishops. Its purposes are "first, to reaffirm the ethical standards of behavior in

[16] "Pamela Cook: The X Factor Australia 2011 Audition," HipToeKnee, August 30, 2011, YouTube video, https://www.youtube.com/watch?v=d26i_2Hsngs.
[17] "Pamela Cook," YouTube video.

health care that flow from the Church's teaching about the dignity of the human person; second, to provide authoritative guidance on certain moral issues that face Catholic health care today."[18] A review of several of their positions align with Pamela's decisions. For example, in Article 45, they write,

> Abortion (that is, the directly intended termination of pregnancy before viability or the directly intended destruction of a viable fetus) is never permitted. Every procedure whose sole immediate effect is the termination of pregnancy before viability is an abortion, which, in its moral context, includes the interval between conception and implantation of the embryo.[19]

By refusing abortion, Pamela made a decision in line with this. Now let's look at Article 47:

> Operations, treatments, and medications that have as their direct purpose the cure of a proportionately serious pathological condition of a pregnant woman are permitted when they cannot be safely postponed until the unborn child is viable, even if they will result in the death of the unborn child.[20]

---

[18] United States Conference of Catholic Bishops (USCCB), Ethical and Religious Directives for Catholic Health Care Services, 6th ed. (digital ed., June 2018), 4, https://www.usccb.org/resources/ethical-religious-directives-catholic-health-service-sixth-edition-2016-06_0.pdf.

[19] USCCB, *Ethical and Religious Directive*, 18.

[20] USCCB, *Ethical and Religious Directive*, 19.

This is where the "Principle of Double Effect" is often referenced, which involves doing a good (or neutral) act that can have both good and bad effects (hence the label "Double Effect"). Treating a pathology of a pregnant woman is good. And that can have two effects: a good one of helping the pregnant woman and a possible bad one of harming the child. In Pamela's case, because she had the pathology of cancer in her body, it was ethical to pursue chemotherapy. It was not being administered to kill her baby but was being administered to kill her cancer. In her case, the chemotherapy did not end her child's life, but there came a point where it was decided her baby should be delivered early.

This is where Article 49 is also relevant: it says, "For a proportionate reason, labor may be induced after the fetus is viable."[21] This shows there is a balancing act between treating a mother's condition to preserve her life and making the best decision about what will help a baby's life (whether to stay in the womb or to be in an incubator).

From this story and analysis, we can deduce that whatever is "broken" in a woman's body, whether it is something pathological in her body or something pathological with how the pregnancy is unfolding, we must look for solutions that are corrective to the pathology itself. But we must never view the child as a pathology. The word "pathology" connotes disease—something gone wrong, a deviation from the norm. Pathology is what

---

[21] USCCB, *Ethical and Religious Directive*, 19.

we experience in this broken world, and that's why the aforementioned directives allow for some interventions as long as we orient those interventions to addressing the problem that has arisen, not to directly ending a life itself.

Inevitably, people might be thinking of other conditions that can arise and how the principles would apply—especially as to what would and what would not fall under the "Principle of Double Effect." Because this is not a bioethics textbook meant to go in depth on the varied medical dilemmas that can arise in pregnancy, I draw the reader's attention to the National Catholic Bioethics Center (ncbcenter.org), which provides personal consultation services to people facing, or involved with, medically and ethically complex situations.

Returning, then, to the case studies to be examined here, as Pamela's story reveals, if cancer treatment should not be delayed, it is ethical to pursue; having said that, one could still choose to delay further. That is the story of another woman: Lorraine Hall.

Like Pamela, Lorraine was also in her late twenties and was also around four months pregnant when she was diagnosed with breast cancer. She was told it was a very aggressive type, one that would metastasize quickly. A doctor told her and her husband that they needed to end the pregnancy immediately so she could begin treatment. Lorraine simply responded, "No, I can't do that."[22] The doctor replied, "No. You don't understand. You have a

---

[22] This and other quotes and details about Lorraine's story are taken from an interview of Lorraine's husband, Darrell, conducted by Stephanie Gray Connors on November 16, 2022.

very aggressive form. If you don't begin treatments immediately, it will likely cost your life. The longer you wait, your survival chances go from slim to none." Lorraine replied, "No. You don't understand. I could never kill my child. I'll take my chances."

She carried through with the pregnancy, delivering her daughter, Erin, at full term. After Erin's birth, they began cancer treatment, which included surgery, chemotherapy, and radiation. Initially her cancer seemed to go into remission, but then it came back with a vengeance. Baby Erin turned two in October 1985, and the following month, Lorraine got really sick. By that point the cancer had metastasized throughout her body, and no treatment could eliminate it. One month later, she passed away.

Had Lorraine pursued treatment earlier would she be alive today? We will never know, but Lorraine's husband Darrell said, "Lorraine was very steadfast about the importance of this child to her; that child was more important than life itself." Lorraine certainly maximized the odds of protecting her child's life.

Darrell knew that one day, he would have to explain to his daughter how her mom had sacrificed her life for her, and when that day came, Erin said matter-of-factly,

Dad, don't worry. Michael [her brother] and I have already talked about this. We already know what happened. I know what my mom did for me. I'm okay, Dad; I'm okay. I want you to know, for me, my whole life is going to be about honoring her sacrifice. She gave birth to me. She gave me life. I just want to be a mom and give life to other kids.

And she has. Erin has four children and, like her older brother, loves the Lord and has remained steadfast in her Catholic faith. In reflecting on his wife, Darrell reminded me of Matthew 6:19–21:

> Do not lay up for yourselves treasures on earth, where moth and rust consume and where thieves break in and steal, but lay up for yourselves treasures in heaven, where neither moth nor rust consumes and where thieves do not break in and steal. *For where your treasure is, there will your heart be also* [emphasis added].

Darrell said, "Where was Lorraine's heart? It was with the baby in her womb. That was of ultimate value." He described his wife as having what he calls "the unbeatable three: courage, love, and the willingness to suffer." He explained, "The love she had for the child in the womb is what gave her the courage to be willing to sacrifice herself." These three qualities, he explained, summarize what our faith represents—it's exactly what Jesus did. Darrell said, "The love Jesus had for us is what gave Him the courage to be willing to sacrifice Himself."

Lorraine, Darrell pointed out, did everything our faith calls us to do: "The two greatest commandments we are given are to love God and to love our neighbor, and she did that. I think Jesus was looking down and was so pleased with Lorraine," Darrell said, "because when she was presented with an opportunity, she chose to live her life for God and for other people. I think Jesus was smiling and saying, 'There's one of my daughters that really understands me and understands the faith.'"

Both Lorraine and Pamela loved their children. Both of them refused physician counsel to commit homicide on the youngest of our kind. Both of them ultimately sought treatment for their illness with the hope they would be alive to mother their children. Could Lorraine have chosen a path like Pamela and pursued cancer treatment *earlier* than she did? She could have, and that would have been ethical. But even if she had, we have no guarantee it would have saved her life. What we are guaranteed is that Lorraine had the right disposition. Precisely because her story does not end, on this earth anyway, as a "happily ever after," it is worth highlighting.

Perhaps childhood fairytales have built within us an expectation that everything always ends as we want. But it doesn't. Lorraine's story is a powerful reminder to us, as we have observed repeatedly in this chapter, that our goal in life is not length of life; our goal is heaven.

An older friend of mine recently shared with me that decades ago, her sister was killed in a car accident, leaving behind a husband and three young children. How can one explain that sort of suffering and loss? It's hard to, unless we live with an eternal perspective—namely, that this earth is not our home. We are pilgrims on a journey learning about love and to love so we can live forever in perpetual light. Neither Lorraine, Pamela, nor any of us has any guarantee of living until one hundred. If it's not cancer that ends someone's life, it could be a car accident, a heart attack, or something else. Just because someone has made it to their late twenties doesn't mean they will live until their late thirties, let alone their late nineties. And so, ethically demanding situations like Pamela's and Lorraine's are actually profound opportunities to orient ourselves to our ultimate purpose (love) and to our ultimate home (God in heaven).

It is worth returning, then, to more of Lorraine's story. Her husband shared with me that as her health rapidly declined in November 1985, her wish was to live for one more Christmas. Mercifully, she did. On December 25, 1985, she was awake for an hour total, and although she couldn't get out of bed and wasn't entirely lucid, Darrell brought the children to her, and she opened presents with them. The next day she said to him, "Is it Christmas yet? Did I miss Christmas?" and Darrell reminded her of the previous morning together with the children. With a huge smile, she said, "Oh, yes!" Just hours later, she died.

I think it was no accident that Lorraine lived to another Christmas. The feast of Christ's birth is so significant to Lorraine's own story. As Mary labored for Jesus and lived out *"This is my body given for you,"* Lorraine had done the same in labor and in her decision to preserve Erin's life. Jesus was born so that we might live, and Lorraine delayed treatment and gave birth so that her daughter might live. Jesus was willing to die for us, and Lorraine was willing to die for her daughter. "Take up your cross and follow me," Jesus said. And Lorraine responded, "Amen."

I also think it was no accident that she entered into eternal life on the feast of St. Stephen, who was stoned to death as the first Christian martyr. What do he and all other martyrs demonstrate? That our goal is not length of life; it is heaven. Martyrs do not hold onto their lives at all costs. They do not want to gain the whole world if they will lose their soul in the process (Matt 16:26). Martyrs live by the belief that doing the right thing is always the right thing. They take on a heavy cost but receive a greater reward. They live by *memento mori*. That's a Latin phrase meaning "remember that you must die," and for centuries, it is a phrase that has oriented human beings to the fact that death is everyone's fate. If we remembered our impending death more often, we would live a life of love and commitment to Christ.

Now it is worth pointing out that death wasn't supposed to be part of the human story. And it wasn't so "in the beginning." But because we live in a fallen world, death became a reality that unites everyone. It is good to work to save lives from death because God is a God of life. (That's why we support building hospitals and we grieve concentration camps.) Even Jesus healed people from ailments. But His *ultimate goal* was not physical healing—it was spiritual healing. While we should never intentionally bring about death, we also cannot ward it off forever, so our focus should be on *eternal* life, and *that* is what should guide our decision-making in this life.

In our western world of longevity, many medicines, and impressive healthcare, we tend to not think so much about the inevitability of death. And then, when it does come to the forefront of our minds, we often respond with fear. In fact, the world's response to COVID-19 highlighted this. People were so singularly focused on avoiding death that, on many occasions, we lost our humanity. We separated ourselves from loved ones, embraced isolation, attached ourselves to devices, and left the sick and elderly to languish alone—all because we were afraid of death. It was as though we lost sight of our goal of heaven and instead focused on length of life.

But as Lorraine's story teaches us, it is better to live a shorter life filled with love than a longer life marked by self-centeredness. The brokenness of our bodies thus becomes a reminder of the need for the salvation of our souls.

A Post-Roe Application

In September 2022, the *Dr. Phil* television show featured a story about a woman from Louisiana who had been pregnant with a child who had acrania. This condition meant her baby had not developed a skull around his or her brain and would die shortly after birth, if not before. The woman said that upon learning this news at ten weeks of pregnancy, her doctors advised her to have an abortion, and she wanted to pursue that path. Her story became public when her doctors initially told her that they would not do the procedure for fear they could be breaking a new law in Louisiana that had almost entirely restricted abortion access after the Dobbs decision. She ended up traveling out of state to New York to have her pre-born child killed at sixteen weeks of pregnancy. She said, "I was carrying my baby to bury my baby."[23]

The reality is that every mother carries her baby to bury her baby because every single child who is born will ultimately die. Granted, usually children outlive their parents, so generally, it isn't our mothers who bury us, but it is our mothers who bring us into a world where we will ultimately face death and burial. We mustn't forget this because no mother has any guarantee about the length of her child's life. We should love our children for who they are, not for how long they live.

When people support abortion for a poor prenatal diagnosis, we should ask, *When our babies' bodies are broken, may we parents break their bodies even further? When our children are sick, does that give us license to rush their lives away?* Had that woman's child been given the chance to live until dying naturally, the baby would have died from acrania. In the end, however, the baby did not die from that rare condition. Instead, the child died by being directly killed through abortion.

There is no denying the anguish the mother would have gone through if her child had died at birth. Her choice to have an abortion, however, did not prevent her from the experience of losing her child; instead, it changed *how*

---

[23] Dr. Phil McGraw, "Carry to Bury: The Abortion Debate," *Dr. Phil*, September 12, 2022, YouTube video, https://www.youtube.com/watch?v=fcVuPQ2xX_A&t=1365s.

she lost her child. Tragically, instead of her child's life ending through no fault of her own, she has to live with the reality that her child died at her own hand.

I think of my friend whose husband has cancer and has been given an estimate of six months left to live. He and his wife are savoring the time they have left, visiting family and friends, praying, living and loving until his life ends naturally. How sad and strange it would be if his wife said, "If I can't have you for twenty more years, I don't want you for the next six months. Let's just end your life now." And yet that's essentially what people like this woman from Louisiana convey by their actions—*if I cannot have a full life with my child, then I want no more life with my child.*

Instead of terminating one's baby, what should be terminated is that type of sentiment. And in the remaining, challenging time that is left, parents facing bleak prenatal diagnoses can be supported and uplifted through programs like perinatal hospice, as explained in Chapter 3, as well as by family, friends, and community. Let us continue on with an eternal perspective marked by love for both mother and child.

8

When Our Bodies Are Protected

She gazed through the wall of windows
As afternoon sun gleamed
To notice the love of a father
Digging
His daughter's grave
To lay his first baby to rest
To enclose her tiny body
In an earthen tomb

———

He dug
Deeper into the soil
And into his soul
A father shouldn't have to bury his child
But at least his child wouldn't have to bury her father

I wrote these poems on a bright, sunny day as I watched my husband dig four feet into the ground to prepare a grave for our first child. LaeLae's coffin was a tiny cigar box because she was the youngest of our kind, having left us through miscarriage.

Dr. Martin Luther King Jr. once said, "The ultimate measure of a man is not where he stands in moments of comfort and convenience, but where he stands at times of challenge and controversy."[1] Miscarriage early in our marriage was indeed a time of great challenge for my beloved husband and me. It was he whose strong frame was my rock as I leaned into him, moaning through mini-labor pains of contraction as my body expelled our child and all that had nourished her. When the gestational sac that held the tiniest, most concealed of bodies fell into the toilet, it was my husband who retrieved it, knowing that hidden within was a miniscule body that had homed a soul. He sprinkled holy water, baptizing LaeLae in the name of the Father, and of the Son, and of the Holy Spirit, because he saw with the eyes of his heart.

Her earthly father had loved her with tenderness and reverence and sent her soaring to her Heavenly Father's sanctuary until the day we meet again. In every way, my husband showed himself to be father. He had protected, provided, and prayed over our little one. And when he could do nothing to preserve her body in this broken world, he was oriented to the good of her soul.

That was the role of a father in miscarriage. But what is the role of a father in abortion? All too often it is one of abandonment. Instead of rescuing those being dragged to the slaughter (Prov 24:11), all too often, a father's role in abortion is to drive a pre-born child to death, delivering him or her and the child's mother into the hands of a doctor who betrays his profession. The

---

[1] Martin Luther King Jr., *Strength to Love* (Boston, MA: Beacon Press, 1963), 26.

relationship of man to woman and of parent to child was not meant to be like that.

Back when I was single, I attended a Mass where one of the hymns we sang was "The Servant Song." I took a photo of the lyrics to remember what I wanted to have in my future marriage. It reads, in part, "Will you let me be your servant, let me be as Christ to you? . . . We are here to help each other walk the mile and bear the load."[2] A father who embraces the new life of pregnancy sings "The Servant Song." A father who celebrates the new identity of *"mother"* for the woman he loves sings "The Servant Song." A father who supports and cares for his child and the woman who bonds him to that child through parenthood sings "The Servant Song." A father who grieves the loss of life in the womb that left the world too soon sings "The Servant Song."

In my experiences while growing up, in what I have witnessed working in the pro-life movement, and in my married life now, I have seen countless examples of good men who care for others, whose lives demonstrate the beautiful melody of "The Servant Song." From my own father, to priests who served at my parish, to high school teachers, to men in the pro-life movement who worked on projects alongside me, to my husband, again and again I have witnessed men who stand beside, support, and defend the women and children in their midst.

---

[2]   Richard Gillard, "The Servant Song," Universal Music, Brentwood Benson Publishing, 1977, http://catholichymn.blogspot.com/2016/03/the-servant-song.html.

That's why I've always found it bewildering when encountering abortion supporters who express scathing hostility toward men. I have witnessed their disgust, disregard, and disdain when speaking of men. I do not share their opinions. And then I had a realization—maybe I do not share their opinions because I do not share their experiences. Perhaps they have been deeply wounded by men, whether through abandonment or overt attack. Certainly one cannot describe all men in her life as bad, but perhaps one or several *key* male relationships—a father, a spouse, boyfriend, a brother—are defined by suffering and not safety.

In my pro-life ministry, one of the most Christ-like men I have ever met is Bishop Thomas Olmsted of Phoenix, Arizona. We crossed paths several times over my years of public speaking and maintained a friendship. He became a source of wisdom and a spiritual father to me, so much so that he presided over my wedding. Every time I am with him, I am struck by his humility, gentleness, and reverence. He shows a keen interest in listening to the other and has a masterful ability to demonstrate both meekness as well as firm and holy boldness. In 2015, he wrote a powerful reflection for men titled "Into the Breach." He said,

> At one striking moment of Jesus' trial, Pontius Pilate, with all his worldly power, presented Jesus to the crowd with the words, *Ecce homo*—Latin meaning "Here is the man!" Thinking he was merely pointing to a man from Nazareth, he failed

to recognize that he was pointing to God made man—the Word made flesh, Jesus of Nazareth—who at once is fully God and fully man, and the perfection of masculinity. Every moment of his life on earth is a revelation of the mystery of what it means to be man—that is, to be fully human and also, the model of masculinity. Nowhere else can we find the fullness of masculinity as we do in the Son of God. Only in Jesus Christ can we find the highest display of masculine virtue and strength that we need in our personal lives and in society itself. What was visible in Christ's earthly life leads to the invisible mystery of his divine Sonship and redemptive mission. The Father sent his Son to reveal what it means to be a man, and the fullness of this revelation becomes evident on the Cross. He tells us that it was for this reason that He came into the world, that it is his earnest desire to give himself totally to us. Herein lies the fullness of masculinity; each Catholic man must be prepared to give himself completely, to charge into the breach, to engage in spiritual combat, to defend women, children, and others against the wickedness and snares of the devil![3]

There are some fathers who, when their child is at risk of abortion, *are* willing to be like that. There are men

---

[3] Rev. Thomas J. Olmsted, "Into the Breach," Diocese of Phoenix, September 29, 2015, https://dphx.org/into-the-breach/.

who, rather than drive their child to death, will step into the breach and attempt to rescue those being dragged to the slaughter.

I am reminded of such a man who reached out to me in the early 2000s. He called me because he saw an advertised talk I was going to give on abortion. He shared that his girlfriend was pregnant and wanted an abortion, but he didn't want her to end their child's life. Was there anything he could do to save his baby? Did he have any legal rights?

Sadly, regarding the latter, modern society robbed him of the role of fatherhood that was rightfully his. Regarding the former, he could try to persuade her, but time would tell whether she would be convinced. So try he did, telling his live-in girlfriend that he would marry her. Or that if she didn't want that, he would raise the child by himself. The morning of her scheduled appointment he again tried to convince her of his willingness to stand with and by her and their child. But tragically she went ahead in exercising her legal "right," and his child was no more. He described his feelings that day of being "helpless" and "powerless"—the exact opposite of what a man should be.

Although he now lives with a grief that can never be fully lifted, he made it his life's mission to be a voice for pre-born children. He works full-time in the pro-life movement and has done so for two decades. He continues to step into the breach.

What happens when a father doesn't do that? Some couples may be in the opposite circumstance from above.

In some situations, the man disappears, leaving the woman to feel like abortion is her only option because she feels she has no support. It *is* hard to be pregnant and raise a child without a life partner.

I have reflected on that reality in light of *having* a life partner. My husband is an incredibly present dad, and yet, even with his significant involvement, motherhood has its challenges. I have come to see why this phrase exists: "It takes a village to raise a child." We were made for connection, and we need community—lots of it.

When my husband and I were preparing for Violet's birth, we naively decided we didn't want any extended family (all of whom live many states or a country away) to visit immediately. We had visions of returning home from the hospital and bonding as just the three of us, able to take care of our newest family member, meals, the house, and so forth on our own. Then COVID hit us the week before birth. Then there were post-birth challenges at the hospital along with serious breastfeeding difficulties. The reality of the challenges of taking care of ourselves, let alone for seven wonderful pounds of flesh, prompted us to learn a lesson fast: when you have a baby, you need to take all the help you can get.

My saintly sister offered to fly across the continent with the express purpose, she said, "to serve you." And serve she did. Friends organized a meal train. Even a couple we had never met, who have longed to have children of their own but miscarried the one child they were able to conceive, brought us a meal. With a new little one, we were essentially living their dream, but they were singing

"The Servant Song," too, and were willing to look past their pain to alleviate some of ours.

We continue to grow our village. I have called on more experienced moms for advice on raising a child so that my daughter flourishes. One such mom, incredibly busy with eight children of her own, took the time to listen to me and provide wisdom. The care and love of these others reminds me of Jesus's mother, Mary, and her cousin Elizabeth. When Elizabeth was pregnant and in need of support, Mary, with her own servant's heart, visited her in order to help—all the while she herself was pregnant. And when Mary was preparing to give birth to her own child, she had the faithful support of Joseph, a strong protector by her side. There is a time to give and there is a time to receive.

For the woman who doesn't have a "St. Joseph," she can still create a village. I think of a friend of mine who got pregnant unexpectedly in college and the child's father was completely out of the picture. Her parents and sisters rallied around her, making it possible for her to live well as a single mom. She isn't supported by a spouse, but she is lifted up by helping hands.

Or I think of a college student I met at a pro-life exhibit. She got pregnant at sixteen, and her boyfriend wanted her to get an abortion. Her own father wanted her to get an abortion too. And her five brothers? They stopped talking to her, and she only began to reconnect with them when I met her, at which point her son was a toddler. As for her mom, she died when this young woman was only two years old. Talk about no village. Talk about total abandonment.

But to quote this brave young woman directly, "I seeked help," she told me. She found a pro-life center that ran programs to help pregnant women in need. Through that, she met a couple who invited her into their lives and adopted her. They have been a faithful and steady source of support that has helped her and her son flourish.

When abortion is "off the table," when it is just not an option, then we are forced to look for help we didn't know existed but actually does—once we start knocking. For all the criticism of abortion supporters that "the pro-life movement doesn't care about women or about children after birth," a quick search of pregnancy centers and pregnancy homes will reveal just the opposite. Take, for example, Mary's Shelter. Founded in 2006, they, at the time of this writing, have helped hundreds of women:

> Our program provides women and their children, both born and unborn, with the unique opportunity of living at Mary's Shelter for up to three years in order to further their education and/or secure a career, while also attending in-house parenting and life-skills classes. Each woman is blessed with a mentor who provides hands-on guidance, compassion and support. This foundation ensures women have the necessary time to work toward their goals and provide for their

children, making the possibility of independent, stable living a reality.[4]

Then there's my all-time favorite ministry that steps into the breach and protects and uplifts pregnant women: the Sisters of Life. My connection to them goes way back. In January 1999, I was eighteen years old and took my first cross-country flight without my parents. I flew with one of my UBC friends, Athena, from Vancouver to Toronto, Canada, where we attended a conference for pro-life college students. That weekend changed both of our lives.

The main presenter was an American named Scott Klusendorf, who did hours of training in pro-life apologetics. He equipped us to be winsome and persuasive defenders of the pro-life view and inspired us to make a positive difference in the world. He said a lot that weekend, and although more than two decades have since passed, there is one quote in particular that I have never forgotten: "There are more people working full-time to kill babies than there are working full-time to save them," he said.

Athena and I were profoundly moved by that tragic reality. Abortion clinics had doctors, nurses, and others making it their careers to end babies' lives and advance an abortion-supporting agenda. In contrast, the pro-life movement I had grown up in was largely made up of volunteers and few, if any, full-time employees. That

---

[4] "History," Mary's Shelter, accessed on September 14, 2023, https://marysshelterva.org/history/.

needed to change, and the Holy Spirit convicted Athena's heart and mine to be part of that change.

In May 2001, Athena and I took another flight together, this time to New Jersey to attend a seminar by Scott on the practical aspects of working full-time in the pro-life movement. While on the east coast of the United States, we took a tour of New York City, and Athena seized the opportunity to make a side trip. Besides a passion for the pro-life cause, she sensed the Holy Spirit calling her to discern religious life, and she wanted to visit a new order of nuns in the Bronx called the Sisters of Life.

The year prior, while attending World Youth Day in Rome, she heard God calling her to love Him with an undivided heart. She responded to that prompting and was particularly drawn to this order of religious sisters who take a special fourth vow: to protect and enhance the sacredness of human life.

The Sisters of Life live a life of prayer and service, particularly focused on pro-life issues. They have a mission to help pregnant women and serve women in crisis—even opening the doors of one of their convents to mothers and their children. Athena entered the sisters in 2002, became Sister Antoniana Maria, and professed perpetual vows on August 6, 2010. Since that time, she has served as the Vocations Director, Assistant to the Superior General, the Local Superior of the Motherhouse in New York, and—as of this printing—the Local Superior of the Toronto Convent.

Having visited the Sisters of Life on several occasions over the years, I can testify that it is a beautiful order of women who radiate maternal love that inspires and edifies. When speaking about her vocation call, Sister Antoniana said, "I'm just so grateful to be called to lay down my life so others may live."[5] Once again we see a servant's heart, the fulfillment of self-sacrificing love that is best modelled by Jesus and then reflected through motherhood. Although these religious sisters will never be biological mothers, they are living out the fullness of their femininity by being *spiritual* mothers to many more than one woman could physically generate and attend to. Consider this quote from their founder John Cardinal O'Connor, which captures this sentiment:

> This is the charism of the Sisters of Life: to mother the mothers of the unborn; to mother the unborn; to mother all those who are frail, all of those who are vulnerable, all those who are ill, all of those who are in danger of being put to death, all those whose lives the world considers useless. Our Lord says to each Sister of Life, "Woman, behold your son. Behold your daughter."[6]

The sisters have a policy of "non-abandonment" and journey with a woman after her pregnancy for as long as the woman needs. As good mothers, they know when their

---

[5] Sister Antoniana, "Happy First Sunday of Advent!" Facebook video, November 28, 2021, https://m.facebook.com/vocationstoronto/videos/happy-first-sunday-of-adventsister-antoniana-is-a-member-of-the-sisters-of-life-/434657414786479/.

[6] "Why We Exist," Sisters of Life, accessed on September 14, 2023, https://sistersoflife.org/who-we-are/why-we-exist/.

daughters need to be lavished with love. Yes, motherhood calls forth personal sacrifice; however, just as a car cannot run on empty, neither can mothers. The sisters magnify the feminine genius; they tenderly care for women in need, recognizing that mothers also need to be encouraged, helped, given a break, provided respite, uplifted, pampered, and so forth. The sisters do this beautifully, thoughtfully, and uniquely for each woman they serve.

Another beautiful thing about the Sisters of Life is that they have established a network that expands beyond their own direct involvement with pregnant women. This is a community of people who also give of their time and talent as a way of singing "The Servant Song." They have "Handmaids," whom they describe as "Women with the 'heart of Mary' who befriend a woman in a difficult pregnancy."[7] They have "Visitation Brothers" who are "men who approach the father of the baby with the heart of a brother, mentoring and guiding him in learning to support the mother of his child."[8] They have "St. Joseph's Workers," who are "men willing to help a vulnerable pregnant woman by building cribs, moving furniture, and other 'handy-man' services."[9] They have even networked with families and single women who will open their homes to pregnant women in what is called "Holy Respites." And the list goes on.

---

[7] "Serve with Us: One Heart at a Time," Sisters of Life, accessed on September 14, 2014, https://sistersoflife.org/what-we-do/serve-with-us/.

[8] "Serve with Us," Sisters of Life.

[9] "Serve with Us," Sisters of Life.

This gives much hope to anyone who feels she has no support. There are many people willing to step into the breach and act as spiritual mothers and spiritual fathers to those who need such protective care.

What about situations where the biological parents choose not to raise their children and instead place them for adoption, or what about children in the foster care system? Once again, the pro-life movement steps into this breach. I remember being blown away by the heart of a twenty-eight-year-old woman who worked at a pregnancy care center and whom I met in my speaking travels. She was not married, yet she had fostered twenty-one children and adopted two of them.

Then there's a pro-life leader I worked with who, along with his wife, adopted three girls from China who had severe cleft palate, which required multiple surgeries.

Then there's a couple I met who adopted two children when their first biological child was only one. They have since adopted two more children, both of whom have Down syndrome and serious heart conditions, all the while giving birth to five more children.

Then there's a pastor I met who was in his mid-fifties. He and his wife had already raised their own children and then fostered three children whom they planned to adopt.

Or I think of a pastor of a mega church in Texas who told me he is implementing a program where his church members make it their mission to foster and/or adopt local orphans.

These are just a few examples, of many I know, where people have stepped into the breach to live out the scriptural command "to care for orphans" (Jas 1:27, NABRE).

Finally, in reflecting on when our bodies are protected, I am reminded of a powerful story I came across and what we can learn from it. In June 2019, a father, his seven-year-old son, and the father's friend endured a harrowing, near-death experience.[10] Maike, Julian, and Stephen went fishing off the Caloundra coast in Australia, planning to do something they had done before—an overnight trip, sleeping in their little boat, anchored but surrounded by the vast ocean. In the darkness of the night, their resting bodies awoke to water around them as their boat rapidly sank. For more than six hours, the three souls bobbed amidst the freezing waves, hanging on to two air-filled buckets that just barely kept them afloat. The documentary of their ordeal and the interviews with each person reveal just how close to death they were.[11]

What struck me most was the love of the father for his son. Maike did what he could to preserve his son's life, treading water while holding onto little Julian, who was unconscious for most of the time. When a helicopter finally arrived, Maike's predominant thought was that his son be taken first.[12] Rescue crews assumed Julian was

[10] Matt Doran, "Dad and Son Rescued in Heroic Recovery after Being Lost at Sea for Over Six Hours," 7News, September 24, 2020, https://7news.com.au/sunday-night/dad-and-son-rescued-in-heroic-recovery-after-being-lost-at-sea-for-over-six-hours-c-367706.

[11] Matt Doran, "Dad and Son Survive Shark-Infested Waters for Over Six Hours," 7News, July 29, 2019, YouTube video, https://www.youtube.com/watch?v=w4Tb-3WtFq4.

[12] In an interview, Maike said that if Julian had died in his arms in the ocean, he would have let go and drowned himself because he wouldn't have wanted

dead but did CPR anyway. When he was miraculously brought back to life, they thought he could have brain damage—but he was fine.

Like Maike, a woman in a crisis pregnancy may feel like she's drowning. She may feel overwhelmed by the waves of life crashing around her, seeming to threaten her very existence, and the fact that she's responsible for holding up someone else might just feel like too much to handle. Abortion tempts her to let go. But Maike demonstrates that love enables us to hang on.

When Maike, Julian, and Stephen's boat first capsized, Maike said of his son, "[He] calmed me down. He said, 'It will be alright, dad.' He actually pointed towards Caloundra and said, 'We just have to swim that way, dad.'"[13] They weren't able to swim "that way." But, as the child predicted, everything was alright. Because the father knew to hang on.

And therein lies the lesson for the mother in a crisis pregnancy: to hang on. The child resting beneath her heart needs her, but so, too, does she need others. Abortion eliminates the need for rescuers. Hanging on is what brings into one's sphere a community of rescuers ready

---

to go on living without his son. His emotional reaction is understandable because his love was so great. Having said that, it doesn't mean that such a course of action would have been correct. And so, there lies another lesson here, which is that our ultimate love must be in Creator and not creature. Even when our most beloved of relatives departs from this earth, God still has a purpose for we who are left behind. There are others to love and be loved by, and even when we face excruciating suffering like the loss of a beloved, as Holocaust-survivor and psychiatrist Dr. Viktor Frankl observed, we should seek to find meaning in suffering so as not to despair.

[13] Doran, "Dad and Son Rescued."

to affirm that her life and her child's life are worth fighting for. Whether it is family members, friends, church attendees, pro-life organizations, strangers, or an order of nuns, there *are* protectors who are standing in the breach.

A Post-Roe Application

In states that have banned abortion, there will either be more women needing help carrying through with their unplanned pregnancies or women seeking out abortions in neighboring states. In those states where abortion is allowed, there will still be people who opt for abortion. Therefore, the need to educate, seek political change, and help those in crisis is as important as ever. What does this mean for people of goodwill? What can we do to step into the breach?

In answering that, it helps to reflect on the words of Dr. Martin Luther King Jr. in his "Letter from a Birmingham Jail." He remarked,

> There was a time when the church was very powerful—in the time when the early Christians rejoiced at being deemed worthy to suffer for what they believed. In those days the church was not merely a thermometer that recorded the ideas and principles of popular opinion; it was a thermostat that transformed the mores of society.[14]

14 Martin Luther King Jr., "Letter from a Birmingham Jail," African Studies Center, University of Pennsylvania, April 16, 1963, https://www.africa.upenn.edu/Articles_Gen/Letter_Birmingham.html.

A thermometer versus a thermostat. One tells us the temperature. The other changes it. We need to not only recognize that the temperature needs to change, but we also need to be the ones to change it, channeling any fear we feel into energy that drives change forward.

One way to change the temperature is in the medical community. Physicians, nurses, pharmacists, and others are in positions of great influence and can use their power to educate patients and colleagues on the immorality of abortion and point them in the direction of life-affirming alternatives that involve the practical help of local pregnancy care centers. Medical professionals who are unsure of the ethically sound path to take in a complicated medical circumstance can reach out to the National Catholic Bioethics Center to receive guidance from their ethics consultation line (www.ncbcenter.org).

People could pursue careers in politics, journalism, health care, and other areas to be a pro-life witness within those fields. Alternatively, people could pursue careers directly in the pro-life movement, such as at pregnancy care centers or with educational, political, or activist pro-life organizations.

Pro-life people can also devote their time to volunteering for local pro-life organizations, of which there are many. The faithful commitment of people to their own communities cannot be understated. When I reflect on my own growing-up experience, it involved immersion in all kinds of pro-life activity because of the tireless volunteer efforts of my parents. They brought my sister and me along with them to conferences, rallies, and protests.

Some of their friends were part of the Operation Rescue movement of the 1980s and 1990s, in which pro-life people would peacefully block access to abortion clinic entrances by chaining themselves to entry doors in order to delay openings and dissuade women from pursuing their appointments.

I remember when I was about eight years old helping my parents make placards that said, "Be a hero—save a whale. Save a baby? Go to jail." From a young age, I learned that there were people willing to personally suffer and lose their freedoms to protect pre-born children's lives. I witnessed my mom apply her nursing background to volunteer at the local pregnancy center, helping women and visiting them when their babies were born.

Growing up in the movement, I met so many people who have fostered and/or adopted children in need. I have met so many people whose names will never be honored at banquets but who have made a positive difference in the lives of the vulnerable.

There is no shortage of things we can do to step into the breach. And when we speak, write, and act, we, too, are living out "This is my body given for you." Whatever we do, though, we should bear the following in mind:

1. We need to be constructively critical of our own efforts, asking ourselves questions like *Is what I'm doing bearing good fruit? Is there something I could do to bear better fruit, and more of it?* These questions are important in

ensuring we do not step into the breach to *feel* good but instead to actually *do* good.

2. We should ground all our action in prayer, realizing that God sees the bigger picture and that we need to rely on His inspirations and strength: "Abide in me, and I in you. As the branch cannot bear fruit by itself, unless it abides in the vine, neither can you, unless you abide in me" (John 15:4). We should not underestimate the power prayer has on our careers, volunteer work, and activism, as well as the power of prayer for the conversion of abortion supporters. I think, for example, of the many life-saving testimonies from the 40 Days for Life campaign of prayer and fasting.

3. Whatever we do is likely to rock the boat because many people still believe abortion is a woman's right, and they will, therefore, be offended by our efforts to say otherwise. We will need courage. Consider what we ask of women in crisis pregnancies who want abortion. We ask them to let go of control. We ask them to consider the long-term effects of their choices, not just the short-term. We ask them to not create a false dilemma where it's either "a" *or* "b"—that sometimes "c, none of the above," can be their story. We ask them to do the right thing even when it's hard.

We ask them to remember that it is better to suffer evil than to do evil.

And so, for the pro-life person who is nervous about rocking the boat, we need to personally heed those same messages about letting go of control, having a long-term focus, resisting false dilemmas, and doing the right thing even at the cost of personal sacrifice.

Conclusion

The gardener brought me a flower
Fragile and tall
He told me to keep it
And tend to it all
To watch with wonder
At unfolding leaves
To water and fertilize
So it would bear seeds
To give my attention
Affection and love
To help it thrive
As he watched from above
He told me to notice
Big and little things
To remember special growth
That would happen in spring
He told me that patience
Would need to be mine
To be sure my little flower
Would grow mighty and fine
He told me the seasons
Were there for a purpose
Toil and nurture would bring about surplus

At present the buds are small but bright
I will help them develop
Both day and night
When I gaze at the flower
Its beauty and charm
I commit to preserve it
Protect it from harm

It was March 2022. My daughter was seven months old, and each night, she would wake every hour—or less. That's right. After getting up to feed her, I'd have under sixty minutes to get myself back to sleep before she would wake again to be fed. The sleep deprivation was piling up. I felt like I was losing my mind. My husband can testify that the effects of stolen sleep on my mood were, to say the least, *not nice*. At all. Parenthood has profoundly challenging moments.

It also has endlessly beautiful ones. In fact, I wrote the above poem during one of those moments of reprieve in the season of sleep deprivation.

There's nothing quite like picking up your child and having her nuzzle her head into your neck, letting her body go limp in total surrender to your hold.

There's nothing quite like walking into a room and seeing a massive smile spread across your little one's face.

There's nothing quite like hearing your little one say "Mama," and replying "Yes, Violet?" only to hear her simply repeat "Mama" in the sweetest voice.

There's nothing quite like carefree laughter that you can provoke from your child, who might be shy in the presence of strangers but a total ham in the presence of her parents.

There's nothing quite like talking to your baby while breastfeeding her, mimicking her little hums and coos, which turn into shared laughter—and all the while she smiles and giggles, she manages to hold tight with her latch, making the interaction hilariously adorable.

There's nothing quite like staring at a sleeping baby resting peacefully in your arms.

There are so many sweet moments of tenderness, joy, and connection. These are, however, punctuated by loud tears, stiff bodies that refuse to settle into a car seat, moments of boredom, repetitive reading of simple books, messes to constantly clean, vomit and poop—lots of it— plans that don't go your way, and did I mention the sleep deprivation?

I don't know how I would have survived the sleep challenges if it weren't for the active support of my husband. The first year of his PhD program was so stressful and intense that it induced shingles, but even he admits that parenthood is more challenging than his academic trials.

He and I marvel at the intensity of raising a little person and correspondingly have been so grateful for the camaraderie of each other and of the community around us. I am particularly grateful for his calm, patient, and merciful demeanor.

I must confess I have been impatient and frustrated with our sweet child on occasion. Through motherhood, I regularly rediscover my selfishness and how quick-tempered I am. At times I am haunted (truth be told, the very day I am writing this) by St. Paul's Letter to the Corinthians: "If I speak in the tongues of men and of angels, but have not love, I am a noisy gong or a clanging cymbal" (1 Cor 13:1). Some days, like today, I am tested: "Love is patient and kind. . . . Love does not insist on its own way; it is not irritable or resentful" (1 Cor 13:4–5), and I am confronted by my sins. I cannot do the challenge of motherhood alone, and thankfully I don't. And then my mind wanders to those for whom companionship, community, and help are hard to find.

For all my pro-life convictions that we ought not choose abortion, it doesn't mean the pro-life position is an easy path. It is hard because parenthood is hard. Sometimes it is very hard. Then throw complicated relationships or circumstances into the mix, and it might be outrageously hard. We should not minimize the potential hardship involved. While acknowledging the intensity of one's circumstances, we need to ask a question: *In the face of hardship, how* ought *one respond?* In other words, we are not to consider what we *can* do (as any response is *technically* possible), but instead, we are to consider what we *should* do.

The thesis of this book is that love is always the right path, that caring for the lives of our children is always the right thing to do, and that homicide of our offspring is always the wrong thing to do. We should embrace "This is my body given for you" while we reject "This is your body taken for me." As we noted in the previous chapter, there is an abundance of help and support for living out this call to love.

In the 2015 live action remake of the Disney classic *Cinderella*, the main character, Ella, loses her mother as a young girl. Before the mom passes away, she gives Ella this advice: "I have to tell you a secret that will see you through all the trials that life can offer. Have courage and be kind."[1]

Life indeed offers many trials to Ella. Not only does her mother die, but her father marries a woman who, along with her daughters, is wicked to Ella. Ella's father then dies, leaving Ella in the hands of three women who treat her with brutality and contempt. Ella faces so much hardship, but she heeds her mother's advice and remains virtuous throughout.

Although the story is a fairytale, it is, on another level, the story of so many. How many women (or men) face one trial after another? It can be tempting when we are victims of misfortune, hardship, and injustice to think we are granted license to behave badly in response.

This is a point I raised in one of my debates against Dr. Malcolm Potts. From 2015 to 2018, I shared a stage with him on several occasions in front of his students at the University of California, Berkeley. Although he ultimately landed a job as a professor there, previously he had been the first medical director for International

---

[1] *Cinderella*, directed by Kenneth Branagh (Burbank, CA: Walt Disney Studios Motion Pictures, 2015), 106 min.

Planned Parenthood Federation and had a long history of performing abortions.

After several occasions of hearing his arguments and interacting with his students, I felt that one message I needed to get across was to acknowledge that hardship in unplanned pregnancies is real while imparting the principle that we still have a duty to act morally.

To make this point, I drew on the insights of psychiatrist and Holocaust-survivor Dr. Viktor Frankl. In his book *Man's Search for Meaning,* he wrote about some survivors who, having been surrounded and hurt by brutality and cruelty for so long,

> thought they could use their freedom licentiously and ruthlessly. The only thing that had changed for them was that they were now the oppressors instead of the oppressed. They became instigators, not objects, of willful force and injustice. *They justified their behavior by their own terrible experiences* [emphasis added]. This was often revealed in apparently insignificant events. A friend was walking across a field with me toward the camp when suddenly we came to a field of green crops. Automatically, I avoided it, but he drew his arm through mine and dragged me through it. I stammered something about not treading down the young crops. He became annoyed, gave me an angry look and shouted, "You don't say! And hasn't enough been taken from us? My wife and child have been gassed—not to mention everything

else—and you would forbid me to tread on a few
stalks of oats!"

Only slowly could these men be guided back to
the commonplace truth that no one has the right
to do wrong, not even if wrong has been done
to them [emphasis added]. We had to strive to
lead them back to this truth, or the consequences
would have been much worse than the loss of a
few thousands stalks of oats.[2]

There are certainly some who could rightly say wrong
has been done to them, such as victims of rape or a
woman abandoned by her baby's father. Then there is a
myriad of other circumstances that are really hard—like
a child with a disability or a complicated health condition or having minimal support. These tough situations
can make some feel justified in pursuing "termination."

But the life that would be terminated is one that had
already begun, starting at fertilization. And that little
body isn't just any little body—it's the living body of
one's own offspring. Parents, and mothers in particular,
have a grand calling to devote their very bodies to the
sustaining of their child's life, and to quote Frankl again,
"no one has the right to do wrong, not even if wrong
has been done to them."

When people lack the relationships or resources they
need to help them be mothers and fathers to their children,

---

[2] Victor Frankl, *Man's Search for Meaning* (Boston, MA: Beacon Press, 1992),
    112–13.

the pro-life position is simply that homicide should never be a solution. Certainly, we ought to respond to those who are struggling with parenting their pre-born or born children. For some, choosing adoption might be their path. For others, getting connected to a church, a non-profit, community support services, friends, or family will be their response. The key we need to promote is help—as highlighted in the previous chapter—not harm. Moreover, we need to show people that this way really is the better way.

That brings to mind a speaking engagement I had mere months before the world shut down due to COVID-19. In November 2019, I traveled to Puebla, Mexico, to participate in a history-making event. I was one of eight women debating the abortion issue in front of thousands at *La Cuidad de las Ideas* (CDI, a festival similar to *TED Talks conferences*). The talk was live streamed to tens of thousands as well as televised throughout Mexico.

Prior to the event, I had prayerfully reflected about what I should impart during my segments of the debate. I nestled into a small adoration chapel in my then-home of Vancouver, Canada, to ask God what He wanted me to say: "Speak, for your servant hears" (1 Sam 3:10).

Of all the ideas that came to mind, two in particular stood out. First, I recalled the message from the "Opposites" video I mentioned in Chapter 5—that the opposite of the greatest love is abortion—and how it relates to abortion. In some way, I knew I had to use that. The second was to associate every hearer's physical body with my message so they would constantly be reminded of the truth proclaimed. For all the differences between us humans, a "tie that binds" is our bellybuttons, and each time people noticed theirs, I wanted them to recall that we were all once in the womb.

With those ideas percolating, I prepared my sixty-second conclusion. It was a profoundly tight window to make my point, so I had it rehearsed down to the second. Except two things happened:

1. The day before the debate, I was inspired by another presenter, Tal Ben Shahar, a professor who teaches the most popular course at Harvard on positive psychology, which is all about happiness. He talked about a psychology experiment in which people were given money and told to buy themselves something, and then their mood/happiness was measured afterward. Similarly, another group of people were given money and told to donate it to someone or some cause, and that second group showed longer-lasting happiness.

    He then used that point to reference something from his first language, which is Hebrew. He said that his favorite name is "Natan," a palindrome that is spelled the same forwards as backwards. He said it means "to give," and his message was that when you give, you also receive. When I heard that, I just knew I should reference him (and his well-received talk) in my closing arguments the following day and use his popular perspective to show how it aligns with a pro-life worldview. Somehow I needed to add more to my already tight conclusion.

2. When the time for the debate came, and as it was nearing its end, with no warning, the moderator shaved down our conclusion from sixty seconds to a mere thirty.

How do you take such a weighty topic and distill your position to half a minute of expression? The old adage "say one thing and say it well" was more relevant than ever. But somehow, in half the time, along with an additional point to make, I was about to say three things. How was that possible? All I can think is that I had asked my prayer team to pray "for a supernatural multiplication of the minutes and seconds in the short timeframes we have to speak," and that prayer was answered. As I watched my precious seconds disappear on the counter, I said,

Every single one of us, on our bodies, has a belly button. Which is a reminder that every single one of us was once a child in the womb. We were once weak and vulnerable and our powerful mothers could have decided to dominate and destroy us by saying, "This is your body given for me." But instead, in an act of love, our mothers said, "This is my body given for you." It's what Tal said—"Natan"—to give is to receive.

Before that conclusion, my opponents had lived true to form by espousing their movement's mantra of "My Body! My Choice!" Rather than entirely reject their sentiment, I opted to define it. When it comes to abortion, it *is* about choice—a choice between two worlds. A choice between a world where (1) people use and abuse each other by selfishly demanding, "This is your body taken for me," or where (2) people reverence and honor each other by selflessly offering, "This is my body given for you."

Of course, these worlds are not new. Throughout human history, there is a dark pattern of sin by which people hurt each other. But over two thousand years ago, a person who was to grow up to become a Jewish rabbi entered our broken world as a pre-born child. He, too, would bear on His body a bellybutton. He would be Son, but He would also be God. And as God, He would continue to do what the Father had always done for His chosen people: He would continue a pursuit of the creation that was "very good" in order to win their hearts to the home of the Father, Son, and Holy Spirit.

But the gates to that home needed to be opened because sin had closed them. The punishment for man's sin was death, but instead, this rabbi, Jesus, would take their place. He, an innocent, would take on the consequence for the guilty. He would offer, "This is My body given for you."

And in that offering was an invitation—a proposal: to choose the greatest love over its opposite. So as we forge ahead in this tumultuous post-Roe world, let us choose. But let us choose well.

Acknowledgments

To Melissa Girard: You have been a cheerleader for this book from the beginning. I was most moved by your willingness to help me with the manuscript even if I didn't land with Emmaus Road Publishing. That spoke to your great character. I am glad that I did land with Emmaus and believe the book has been made better by your insights and contributions as well as all you did to draw new content out of me. You are a fantastic editor and I hold deep gratitude for your belief in this book.

To Caroline Rock: Your great copy editing tightened and refined my manuscript. Thank you! It takes skill to edit while still maintaining the author's voice, and you did that masterfully. I am indebted to your improvements of the fine details of this book.

To Kate Ternus: I am thankful for your graceful refinements of key elements and keen attention to detail and tone. I also hold great gratitude to you for your thoughtful questions, which prompted important revisions.

To Claire Dwyer: We have never met, but your "Prayer for Writers" has put words to the desire of my heart on the many occasions I sat down to write this book. You captured it so well when you wrote, "May my words be the means by which the world receives again and again the staggering story of its salvation and sanctification. May my writing always magnify the message of the Gospel, the Living Word, and draw others to Christ. And may You, Oh God, be praised and glorified in both my words and deeds, now and forever." Thank you for giving me such beautiful words to pray.

To my parents: You have been my living witnesses of our ultimate end of parenthood and of our call to unconditional love. It was you who introduced me to the pro-life movement and demonstrated for me how to serve. Thank you.

To my husband, Joe: Long before we met, you have been a faithful believer and supporter of the pro-life movement and message. You have continued that by giving the gift of your time so that I could give the gift of mine. Every day you demonstrate laying down your life for our family. Thank you. I am, and will be, forever grateful that you are my blueprint.

To the King of Kings and Lord of Lords: "You have the words of eternal life" (John 6:68). With gratitude for Your Holy Spirit breathing life into this book. May You be glorified.